NE

NEVER ALONE

BY

RICHARD E. LESH

EDITED BY

EMILY J. GORMLEY

www.bookstandpublishing.com

Published by
Bookstand Publishing
Morgan Hill, CA 95037
3096_4

ISBN 978-1-58909-701-8

Printed in the United States of America

ACKNOWLEDGEMENTS

Over the years, there have been many people whom I have known and with whom I have shared my many exploits. Many of those same people encouraged me to pen my story; too many to single out. As I figured everyone in my generation had a story equally inspiring in its own right, I never really thought this would be something to do. But, as I aged, the more I thought about the idea, the more I came to believe this book would be something to hand down to my family, something they may read as a source of encouragement.

The only legacy I have ever known was that of my grandfather, and, despite having very little knowledge of him, it is a legacy I hold dear. Perhaps this book can serve as a legacy of sorts for my family in future generations.

I would hope as people read this, they will see the message more than the messenger. As I wander down the last road of my life, I realize mine has been a life profoundly touched by a great many people. It is sad knowing most of those instrumental people are now gone and cannot read how they, with their unbeknownst kindness, had a hand in molding the man I am today.

To those people who are gone, and to those who are still alive today, I dedicate this book.

I accepted my life as normal. After all, what did I know? I was born into the tail end of the Great Depression. An unwanted child, I'd been beaten, neglected, threatened, ridiculed – you name it, I lived it. I learned to survive from an early age, vowing that I would never be abused again, physically or mentally, vowing that I would never be abusive.

I was raised Catholic, but it was my grandfather, a half-breed Indian, who shaped my thoughts about a supreme being. He referred to God as "the great spirit." Who was I to question him? I believe the great spirit of my grandfather has stayed with me throughout my life. I believe I have felt his presence and heard his voice, calming me at the times when I needed him the most. I believe God has been using my grandfather as a channel, as my guardian angel, to lead me safely through life's great adventures. I would like to continue that legacy, and to believe, when my time comes to experience the greatest adventure of all, God will allow me to be someone else's guardian angel.

******

Probably no other event in the history of nuclear power in this country has had such an enormous impact on society, not to mention the industry itself, as the accident that took place at Three Mile Island that fateful day in March of 1979. It has been over 30 years since that day; a lot has happened to the nuclear industry. From that event came new safeguards, new training procedures, new technology in controlling devices, and the moratorium on building new plants. As I look back, I think we must have *really* been at the forefront of nuclear power; you would have thought all these *new* procedures should have been in place from the beginning. Of course, that is pure hindsight, which, as we know, is never wrong.

I have chronicled my involvement from the de-con perspective of the accident at Three Mile Island. I have tried to give you the story you may not have read, or even cared to read at the time. In doing so, I have had the opportunity to step back and explore the personal impact this event has had on my own life. From the memories it sparked to the days it foreshadowed, putting pen to paper to relive my de-con efforts has allowed me to identify the experiences, lessons, and inspirations that have made me the man I am today. It is with these thoughts that I will take you, dear reader, on the journey of my life. Bear in mind, I am just an ordinary person who has lived through extraordinary circumstances.

******

My philosophy is simple. I believe we will all have hardship in our lives, whether the hardship falls at the beginning, the middle, or the end. I believe hardship is the fire that tempers the steel in your backbone. I believe you make your own luck; only you can put yourself in the position to receive good or bad. I believe self-pity is a waste of your inner being; the inner being is better practiced by shaping your destiny. I believe the word "can't" is a crutch to those who are not willing to try their hardest.

******

March 28, 1979. 4:00 A.M. It was bleak and damp outside; the island was shrouded in mist from the cold river. The operators on shift had just poured a cup of coffee. Little did they know they would soon be embroiled in an event that would forever change their lives.

A failure was suddenly experienced in the secondary system, the non-nuclear section of the plant. A main feed water pump had stopped running, either from an electrical failure or a mechanical one; the steam generators were prevented from removing heat. In turn, the turbines shut down. Then, the reactor automatically shut down. The operators were not fully alert; the lethargy of the early morning hours had only just begun to lift. Meanwhile, all hell was breaking loose around them...and they were not exactly sure at that very moment as to what was really happening.

When the reactor shut down, the pressure was increased in the primary system, the nuclear section of the plant. To prevent the pressure from becoming excessive, a pilot-operated relief valve opened. This valve should have closed when the pressure had decreased by a certain amount, but it did not. A faulty valve signal available to

3

the operator failed to show the valve remained open. The resulting cooling water poured out of the open valve, causing the core[i] of the reactor to overheat. As the coolant[ii] continued to flow from the core through the pressurizer, the information provided to the operators by their instruments was nothing short of confusing. Since there was no clear indication the pilot-operated relief valve was open, they did not realize the plant was experiencing a loss of coolant condition. Problems with instruments would prove continuous.

There were also no instruments available to the operators to indicate the level of the coolant in the core. When the plant was constructed, it was assumed such instruments would never be used. The operators were left to their own devices; and human judgment, as we all know, leaves room for human error. They had to judge the level of water in the core by the leveling in the pressurizer; mistakenly, they assumed the core was covered. Amidst alarm bells and flashing warning lights, the operators took a series of actions which made the conditions worse; reducing the flow of coolant through the core only caused inadequate cooling. In turn, the nuclear fuel overheated to the point at which the zirconium cladding[iii] ruptured and began to melt. By the time the accident was under control, 20 tons of fuel had melted – half the fuel in the reactor.

The most feared and dangerous kind of nuclear accident had occurred. The plant had suffered a severe core

4

meltdown.[iv] Fortunately, for all concerned, this accident only served as a necessary wake-up call. The worst case scenario did not happen. Had the core meltdown breached the containment building walls, massive quantities of lethal radiation would have been released into the environment. The proverbial bullet had been escaped. What had been not escaped was the tremendous amount of psycho-physiological damage that would be caused to the public. People living in the area on that fateful day will never forget where they were when they heard about the meltdown.

All hell had broken loose on the island. Realizing they had a possible catastrophic event on their hands, the company tried to downplay the accident as minor and contain the release of information. Finally realizing this strategy would not be possible to maintain, they notified the Nuclear Regulatory Commission (NRC). The federal and state governments were caught off-guard; they were not prepared for the news of such an event. Neither were they prepared to disseminate such news to the public. After all, nothing like this had ever happened before.

Although they were primarily concerned about the discharge of radioactive gases into the atmosphere, the release of James Bridges' *China Syndrome* a mere twelve days before did not make the situation any easier for the governor to handle in respect to his public. This movie told the story of the discovery of safety cover-ups at a nuclear power plant, portending that should an American nuclear power plant suffer a meltdown, it would be so catastrophic that the Earth would continue to melt straight through to China. Hearing the news would bring to mind the movie; people would panic.

The company took immediate steps to gain control of the situation. Without viable assurance there was adequate coolant in the reactor, they decided to shut the reactor down completely. A team of health physics[v] was sent to measure the radiation off-site; several helicopters took flight to measure the radioactivity in the atmosphere. They had yet to learn half the core had melted.

By mid-morning, every NRC headquarters surrounding Pennsylvania had been alerted and sent teams to the site; security was beefed-up. The White House was informed of the accident by 10 A.M.; the order to evacuate the island of all non-essential personnel was delivered less than an hour later.

Nationwide news media were en route to the Middletown area. The island grew eerily quiet for some time. Late into the night, the misty glow of dim lights pierced the relative calm on the banks of the shore. The television stations were having a field day reporting the unfolding event; I remember sitting home watching Walter Cronkite report the story. I don't know how or where they got the very unclear picture of the reactor room so quickly, but the partially-melted red phone in that picture made quite an impression.

Although by midnight it was believed the reactor was under control and the core cooling, becoming stable, new concerns had become apparent. The aux building (auxiliary), which was used to relieve the pressure on the primary system to avoid curtailing the flow of coolant to the core, was now "hot." Unbeknownst at the time, the basement of the building was filled with highly-contaminated water. Not being a sealed compartment, the radiation had begun to escape through the cracks and crevasses in that basement; in turn, large amounts of unmeasured radiation were being released into the atmosphere. The auxiliary had to be sealed as best it could.

The company and the NRC released a statement to the media indicating they were under the guidelines in releasing a minimal amount of radiation from the plant. Concern and confusion were growing about the condition and safety of the island. The governor met with top officials about a full-scale evacuation of the area. It was decided that all pregnant women and small children within a 5-mile radius of the island should be evacuated. The media mistakenly reported the evacuation area as a 50-mile radius; concern was heightened.

To make matters worse, a huge hydrogen bubble had begun to form at the top of the reactor dome.[vi] The possibility of an explosion and consequent rupture of the pressure vessel was quite real. Should that have happened, the core would have fallen into the containment building, causing a breach of containment. In a word, *catastrophic*. Everyone watched and waited; much debate and heated discussion took place throughout that day. The man in charge of the final decision was Harold Denton, President Carter's personal advisor from the NRC. He decided to take a "wait-and-see" approach. Turns out, he was the right man to make that decision; without oxygen, the hydrogen bubble could not catch on fire or explode, it would just slowly dissipate. They waited, they saw.

Calm was somewhat restored to the area by a later visit from President and Mrs. Carter. Although dissent would arise by the "no nukes" crowd again later, for now, routine activity began to resume.

******

Approximately 2.5 million gallons of water were contaminated by the accident on Three Mile Island; that water was stored on the island until it could be processed and evaporated. The processing of this water would not be complete until 1993.

The first human entry[vii] into the reactor room to measure radiation levels was not until July of 1980. The first three-man team with experimental gear to enter the reactor room was in May of 1981. May 14, 1981, to be exact; I remember that date clearly because I was one of the three on that team.

The vessel head[viii] was removed in 1985, the same year the process of defueling was begun; defueling would not be completed until 1990. The first off-site shipment of reactor core debris was seen in 1986.

******

My story is just one of many about the fears and the fates of the men involved with the de-con efforts of the containment building and reactor room on Three Mile Island. Working under extreme conditions, in such a threatening environment, required a great deal of caution and level-headedness. It was both mentally and physically taxing. We were heavily dressed in safety gear, which, for certain entries, included scuba gear. We had to stand, stoop, bend, twist, climb, and handle sharp objects, all the while working without compromise to our safety suits, gloves,[ix] and feet. Claustrophobia could be, and, at times, was, overwhelming. Some team members had to be assisted out; but these men continued to enter the unknown on a daily basis. These were the men I worked with from Met-Ed, the vanguard of future de-con teams. I can't begin to pay proper tribute to every man who worked here, but to the ones to whom I was closest, I will do my best. They were a great group of guys; they deserve special thanks.

******

My experience of Three Mile Island may just be a chapter in my life story, but it is an important chapter. As I told you earlier, recording this experience brought back memories of events and inspirations that span my entire lifetime, both prior to and after my days in de-con. My story is probably not unlike that of many others, but it is an eventful story...it is *my* story.

******

I was born to a dysfunctional family in 1938, at a time devoid of the amenities and luxuries taken for granted today. Can you imagine living in a shack with no lights or water? Can you imagine living with the only heat in your home coming from the kitchen stove? Can you imagine living without indoor bathroom facilities? Can you imagine eating solely off the land? Those were the conditions under which many people lived from the era of the Depression until the beginning of World War II; those were the conditions under which I lived for the first 10 years of my life. The majority of those years I lived with my paternal grandfather. My father was well and working; in fact, he never missed a day's work in his life. He was just drunk and abusive most of the time. Later years would take me in many different directions, exposing me to everything from near-death experiences to the simple pleasures of a traditional family.

All my life I have wondered just how or why I was taken down a road with so many remarkable twists and turns. I have wondered how my journey was driven. Was it by fate? Was it by the will of a higher being? Or, did I have a guardian angel watching over me? Against considerable odds, I have survived some extraordinary circumstances; if I could survive, so can the many other people in this world born into similar circumstances. Perhaps they may read this and take heart, finding the strength and inspiration in their lives so they may live with comparable courage and conviction. Perhaps you, dear reader, may do the same.

******

It was about midnight as I walked down the service road toward the parking lot. The island was dark and foreboding, like a well-designed set from the medieval scene of a movie I'd once seen. The wind was constant, sounding almost like the wail of a banshee[x] as it passed over the top of the cooling towers. Those huge twin cooling towers stood tall, towering, if you will, over the rest of the buildings, like hourglasses cautioning to the essence of time. Their uniquely hyperbolic-curved shape was not without purpose, not just a coincidental warning sign; their shape was designed to provide optimum efficiency in terms of cooling capacity.

The national and historic focus of the accident on this island would surely find itself recounted in every history book written hereafter. Everyone now present on this island was living a part of that monumental history, myself included. I took pause and chuckled to myself; life had held a fair share of excitement for me, but this was certainly a first.

* * * * * *

Turning left across the bridge, I was en route to a Hershey motel near Middletown. I stopped along the way at "Your Place" to see if any of the guys were there. Pulling into the parking lot, I noticed several of their cars; just as I figured. As I walked into the pub, I saw Lou and Tony sitting at a booth. Tony hollered, "Hey, Wahoo! Come on over." Wahoo was the nickname they'd given me because of my grandfather's heritage as a half-breed. That nickname showed up all over the plant, as these clowns wrote it on all the walls; even some of the waste barrels proclaimed "Wahoo was here." I was called in once and told to stop writing on the walls. "Hell," I replied, "it's not me doing that!"

Tony bought me a beer. He was a good man, still down in the dumps from having gone through a bad divorce during the past year. Lou, on the other hand, was still married, but continuously "shopping" for a new love. They would have a confrontation to this end somewhere down the road.

"I hear they have a "hot" job for you," Tony said.

"Probably," I replied. "Jim is coming down next week. The two of us can handle it."

"Yeah, Jim is a bull."

I drank up and hit the road. Crawling into my bed that night, my mind was fully active. I couldn't get to sleep. I began to think back through my life. The troubles Tony and Lou were facing reminded me of my own mother and father.

* * * * * *

January 1941. I was three years old, playing out in snow freshly fallen from the night before. At the time, we were living with my mother's sister and her husband in a two-room, tar-paper shack. My Aunt Anna was dying, though I'm not quite sure why or from what, but I remember seeing the big open hole under her ear with something that looked like worms inside. I remember she was a kind woman; she would hold my hand and tell me stories. I also remember, like it was yesterday, what happened when I came into that house wet from playing in the snow one particular night that January.

After both my mother and my uncle spanked me with a belt, they forced me to stand behind the pot belly stove to dry. I can still see the red ring around the middle; it was so very hot. I was told I had to stand there until my pants had completely dried. My legs were literally burning. When I would cry, they would pull me away from the stove only to spank me again with the belt. Aunt Anna cried out to them to stop more than once, but she could do nothing. I was finally sent to the little crib in which I slept; I could hear Aunt Anna crying as I covered my head with the woolen horse blanket until I fell asleep. That memory is the first of many in the coming years of abuse and neglect. I will never forget those times.

Shortly thereafter, as my aunt lay dying, she would hold my hand and promise to watch over me. I was too young to really fathom her death, but I knew I would miss her.

Not long after Aunt Anna died, I was shipped off to live with my paternal grandfather. My mother moved in with my uncle. They had a child together. To this day, I have never seen him. All I ever heard of the baby boy was that his name was Robert and that he was given away to my uncle's younger sister, who took him to live in Texas.

******

As we rode in the rumble seat of the local horse auctioneer's car en route to his barn, my grandfather explained the horse he was going to talk to had been beaten with a club. Yes, my grandfather could talk to horses. Hearing how that horse had been beaten, I was confronted by a flood of memories from the beatings I'd suffered. I knew how that horse felt.

The horse was tied to a tree; he was a big, golden, high-strung creature who scared me to death. My grandfather pulled me with him toward the monster; the whole time I was trying to pull away. Finally, he stopped, turned to me and, with conviction, said, "Son, don't ever be afraid of anything." Excellent advice, but, at the time, my head was not accepting it. I was beyond afraid. The horse's head was down, ears back, hoof pawing frantically at the ground. I was sure he would bite or kick me. Then, gently, my grandfather began to whisper to the horse. I could not hear exactly what he was saying because I was still trying to keep my distance, staying back as far as I could. As I stood there, I remember hoping my grandfather would not be mad at me for continuing to show fear.

I never wanted to make my grandfather mad; he was the only real father I'd ever known. Yet, I clearly remember making him mad one other occasion. He had told me to get the coal bucket; we were going to walk to the railroad to pick up coal that had fallen along the tracks, coal we would use to heat the house. I was usually eager to walk the tracks, but, that day, I threw a tantrum; I did not want to go. He grabbed me by the nape of the neck and pulled me into the woods. I was so sorry to have upset him, but I was now scared at the same time. Deep in the woods, he told me to scoop out a hole. I thought he was going to bury me. I scratched out some dirt. "Now, young man, get down on your belly and yell into that hole. Then, bury it. We are going to leave your nonsense out here."

My grandfather tried his best to care for me. Things weren't perfect, but they were much better than they had ever been, or would ever be, with my parents. On occasion, he would find broken toys at the dump and bring them home to fix for me.

He taught me so many things in our short time together - how to fish, how to hunt, how to treat the land. "Never take it all, leave some for others," he would say.

I would watch him catching suckers in the creek with his bare hands, standing knee-deep in the water. He would throw one up on the bank; it was my job to catch it. I can honestly tell you, I was scared to death of the fish the first time he did that. As much as I feared that fish would bite me, I knew for certain that not catching it meant having no supper.

He'd set eel lines along that creek; I really loved eel. He would bend over saplings to make snares for rabbits. He taught me to hunt groundhogs with an old, rusty single-shot 22.

******

I had just turned eight. Once again, I found myself holding the hand of a dying beloved. I watched my grandfather as he lay on the couch, smiling. I was crying as he squeezed my hand. "Son, don't ever be afraid. I will always be at your side." He told me I "should be a good boy," closed his eyes, and he was gone.

While I had been living with my grandfather, my parents had gotten back together. It was back to them I was shuffled after his death. From the age of eight to the age of twelve, my life became a blurry hell.

16

* * * * * *

My mind continues to wander back through the many facets of my life. Was it a life determined by fate? Pre-planned, so that I walked blindly down a given path? Might there have been a divine being guiding me… perhaps God channeling through the spirits of guardian angels? I like to believe that of my grandfather, especially, and, perhaps, even my aunt. Maybe God has been using them for me all along, knowing I would listen to them more than a God I had only ever read about in a book? They protected me as best they could when they were alive; I like to believe they continued to do so after they were gone. Life is, after all, but one big circle.

Take, for example, my relationship with the Catholic Church. I was born and raised in the faith, despite the abuse and neglect to which I was subjected as a child. After marrying outside the Church, I was ex-communicated. Then, many years later, I found my retirement years being spent in service to the Catholic Church. Could it be that someone, perhaps a higher power, is trying to tell me something? Could all the twists and turns I've experienced throughout my life have been something more than simple acts of fate? Could it be that my *being* here is more than just an act of fate?

* * * * * *

The first daughter my mother bore died at a mere 6 months of age; by the time I was returned to my parents' home, she had bore a second daughter. Together, we moved with them just about every 6 months, or so it seemed. I felt like I had attended almost every school in every county as far south as Philadelphia.

It was 1947. I can still see the one-room schoolhouse in which I spent my Delaware Water Gap days seated. Each class, or grade, if you will, had a separate row of desks in that schoolhouse. I was in the 4th grade at the time. My desk was right next to the wall. Along that wall was a bookshelf; across that bookshelf was a row of the Encyclopedia Britannica. I can still see quite vividly the big, bold letters on the spine of the volume directly next to my desk — ELECTRICITY. I never thought much about that book at the time, nor about electricity for that matter; but years later I would find myself quite the adept electrician. Now, most people would say there is no meaning to be found here, but I am left to wonder. Was it more than just mere coincidence my desk was in that particular spot? An omen? Perhaps, fated? Was there a thread already looping through my life?

******

With my mom and dad, there was a fight every Friday night. I hated Fridays. They would go shopping. The ride home would be broken up by stops at every bar along the way; stops that would continue until two o'clock in the morning...while I was locked in the car. I would eat cheese and baloney, waiting. After we'd arrive home, they would

18

scream and holler. He would hit her; she would throw dishes at him. I remember being scared, crying until my dad would take his belt to beat me, yelling for me to shut my mouth. Only, he used a particular swear word the entire time; a word I never spoke until I was 19.

The word "love" was never spoken in our house. It would be very difficult for me to say it years later, to my wife. There were no birthdays or holidays in my house. To this day, I don't even know my father's birthday. What I do know is that another coincidental, or, perhaps, fateful, fact of my life is that my wife's birthday just so happens to be the exact same as my mother's.

**

The only redemption during that time was my maternal grandmother. She was from Krakow, Poland, and so spoke very little English. It was always fun to visit her during the summer. Although she was poor, being a devout Catholic, Christmas and Easter were always celebrated in her house. We never had a Christmas tree or presents in ours.

I had many aunts and uncles. My namesake, Uncle Richard, was only three years older than I; he used to get me into so much trouble. Grandma was always asking him to take care of me; time he would spend mostly trying to get me lost.

I remember the first time my grandmother took me to confession. As I set in the cubicle, I heard this deep voice asking me what I had to confess. I was scared to death; I thought it was God! I said, "I don't know. My grandma made me come in here." I heard a muffled laugh before the priest told me to say 10 Hail Mary's.

******

January 27, 1971. A birthday I remember vividly. I was 33 years old, working in the Eastern Division Office. There had been a very bad ice storm. We were trying to get the system up and running. In those days, bucket trucks were not in abundance; we had to climb the poles most of the time. I was standing at the bottom of a 65-foot pole chipping the ice off with my hammer. The pole was solid ice from top to bottom. I had to climb the ice side keeping the opposite, dry side clear for my hands. Digging my hooks into the ice, belting in, I had to continue breaking ice the entire way up, all the while making sure those hooks dug into the pole through the slippery glaze. After some beating and digging, I found myself at the cross arms. I had to un-belt, throw that belt over the arms to bring it around the pole, and, then, re- belt. The cross arms were solid ice. I had to be sure I was in perfect balance and had my hooks in deep. Un-belting again, I threw the belt so it would curl around the top of the arms and the pole, where I caught it with my right hand. It was just then I made the mistake that nearly cost me my life. A foolish mistake, you might say. I took the belt and snapped it into my d-ring. Or, so I thought. In reality, the belt did not snap into the d-ring. My mistake lay in not checking that connection before I made my next move. Thinking I was secure, I began to settle back into the belt. To my surprise, the belt began to come up and slide around the top of the arm and pole.

Scared? You could say that. For one split second, I was near death. That split second was all the time I had to give into my fear, though. Had I fallen backward more than 55 feet down through the air, I would certainly have died. The only thing that kept me suspended at that moment was my right hand. It was clamped over a solid sheet of ice. Had either of the two hooks imbedded in the ice broken free, I would have lost my balance and not been able to recover it.

For that split second, it was as if I was frozen in time. I had to will myself to move. A voice deep inside me said, "Not yet, not the time," and I recaptured my belt. After I had finished the job, climbed down the pole, stored my gear, and gotten into the truck, I poured a cup of coffee. It was then my hands began to tremble. I could not help but think my grandfather had been watching over me. I like to believe he was my guardian angel in that moment, bringing me a sudden calmness, as I hung there, suspended, a brief second from death.

******

It was the middle of January, very cold and snowing. We had moved into a three-room house at the end of a long dirt road, near the railroad tracks and the garbage dump.

We had no electric and no water, but we had an outhouse. My jobs were to chop wood for the stove, keep the water pail full, and get rid of the garbage.

I came home late from Boy Scouts one night that January. It was about eleven o'clock. When I got to the house, all the doors were locked. I could not get inside. I was too afraid to wake my parents. Earlier that month, my dad had brought home a big German Shepherd. Luckily, she had a large dog house. So, that night, wearing only a very thin coat, I crawled into that dog house with her. She kept me warm all night. In the morning, nothing was ever said. I filled the water buckets from the spring about 100 yards from the house; then, went off to school without breakfast. I never really did have a breakfast, just the occasional few pieces of dried bread. In fact, in all the years with my parents, I can remember only one time we ever even sat down together for a meal; it was a supper, pancakes and home fries.

That dog eventually had pups. They were cute little critters. They would wait for me to come home from school every day to feed them. Then, one Saturday, when they were about 2 months old, my dad put them in a box and ordered me to take them down to the dump. I crossed the little bridge, carrying the puppies. My dad hollered for me to put the box down and walk away. I did as I was told. Well, all those puppies jumped from the box and started to follow me. The shots scared me to death. One by one, my father shot them with a 30-30. I gathered

22

them up; it was terrible. Those pups were still warm as I held them. Trying to keep from crying, I found a tin box and buried them away from the dump. My father never said anything about what he'd done. I just accepted what had happened.

******

A doctor's wife once gave me a bicycle her son had outgrown. I was so excited as I rode it home. As soon as my father saw that bicycle, he took it away. He cut the tires and locked it in the cold cellar. He told me that I did not deserve a bike, that I did not work hard enough, and that I was dumb. I never rode that bike again. I was 11 at the time. If I had owned a knife, I thought I might have cut the tires on my dad's car. Of course, he would have known it was me and I'd have been beaten with the water hose yet again.

The next day, I skipped school. With a pocketful of Mary Jane's (you know, the peanut candy), I climbed the mountain to the fire station. I talked to the old man stationed there, then walked back down the mountain in the dark. I slept in a gazebo on the lake. It was the first time I'd tried to run away. I guess I was too scared, because the next day, I went to school and returned home. Nothing was ever said about me being gone the night before.

A year later, my parents separated for good. My mother moved us to town, where we lived in a roach-infested apartment. Funny, my sister lived with us, but I hardly knew her. I was only ever home to sleep. I worked all the odd jobs I could find. The two best were at the local movie theater, where I cleaned up for a dollar and had a free pass to all the movies, and at the local soda fountain, where I was a "soda jerk." They treated me like I was one of their own at that soda fountain. At the age of 15, I was given a lot of responsibility, taking care of the night receipts and closing up shop.

My sister must have had a hard time living with my mother, as my mother was only interested in smoking and in her boyfriends. Incredibly, many years later, another woman called my home and said she was my half-sister. I was, of course, completely unaware my mother had bore another child. I asked my mother about that phone call before she died; she told me it was none of my business. After doing the math, I realized my mother had been pregnant the day I finally left home – the day I joined the Navy.

******

My best friend went to Stroudsburg High School. I was always shy, but he told me he had just the perfect girl for me. She sat in front of him in class. They were in the grade behind me. I never met her, but I received notes from her. To this day, I'm not sure whether she wrote the notes or he did, as I wrote them to her. Her name was Mary Ann. To me, it was love at first sight. She was beautiful, and I knew right away I would never forget her. But, I could just about take care of myself. What could I offer such a girl? I was too embarrassed by my family to be sociable.

In fact, I remember when my class graduated from 9th to 10th grade. There was a formal ceremony, but I had no tie or white shirt. Embarrassed, I sat in the boiler room with the janitor, refusing to go with the other kids. I got my piece of paper from the principal later.

******

Finally, I'd had it with living home. With $5.00 in my pocket, I hitched a ride 35 miles south to Easton. It was the middle of February. I spent one night at the local Y.M.C.A.. The next morning, I went to the post office and enlisted in the Navy. Turns out, it was the best thing I'd ever done. It was the second time I'd tried to run away, and I was no longer afraid. The Navy was my college and my first orderly home. Plus, I got to travel to places no one in my family would ever see.

Fate stepped in during those early days in the Navy. I took the aptitude tests in hopes of becoming a gunner's mate; instead, they sent me to school to become an electrician. Do you remember the big, bold letters on the spine of the encyclopedia shelved next to my desk in grade school? ELECTRICITY.

******

Damn, there is a banging at the door. I open it by mistake and in pile four guys, feeling their oats. "Hey, Wahoo! What are you doing? Have a beer. After next week we may not all be here," they laughed.

I realized I had been flashing back through my earlier years. "I was just reminiscing," I replied. They gathered around, opened a six pack, and handed me a beer. "Reminiscing? What are you trying to remember?" Bill asked.

"Oh, nothing much...just in a melancholy mood, I suppose. I hear next week is going to thin out the herd, so to speak. The testing is pretty tough, and the physical dressing-out procedures are stringent. They say you can hardly breathe in those particulate masks."

"I heard some weird things about the place," Tony replied.

"Like what?" I asked.

"Oh, just the usual rumors and gossip," Tony continued, "like, the place was sabotaged by an inside person who was upset with the company over a promotion. They couldn't find the guy when he left his shift at midnight that night."

"Hell, I can't believe that," I said.

"Why not?" Bill asked. "Anything is damn possible in the company. You know that."

"Yeah, you may be right, but I tend to believe the rumors circulating about a tax break; something about saving money, or getting a big bonus if they got it on-line as soon as possible. Supposedly, they shortened the testing procedures. Even the company would receive a big tax break." Mind you, this was all conjecture among the men on the island, but it seemed to make sense.

"As your shop steward, let me tell you, play it by the book. Watch your ass down here. If you have a problem, bring it to me and we can work it out. Don't let them jerk you around. Each of you, cover the other one's back," I warned.

"Well, you are the closest guy to a nuke man we have, since you had some experience in the Navy," Tony said.

"Hell," I replied. "That was so long ago. I've slept a lot since then and all the experience I had amounted to orientation, not hands on." Those flashbacks were coming on again.

******

My mind wandered back to Newport, Rhode Island, as I remembered the first nuclear sub, the *USS Nautilus*, tied up alongside my work ship on Melville Pier. That was before it made its historic journey under the ice cap. It seems the admiral aboard my ship was friends with their captain. As electricians, we were allowed on board, but never did see the reactor. Was being so close to a reactor that day yet another omen of my future?

******

"Are you afraid, Wahoo?" Bill asked.

"No...are you?" I replied, as I was brought back into the moment.

"No. Just a little leery."

"Well, treat it like high voltage and you'll be fine. I can't stress this enough to you guys - you have to watch out for each other. That is a hostile atmosphere in there. Getting it on your skin is bad enough, but for Christ's sake, don't breathe the damn stuff into your lungs! Remember, everything you touch is contaminated. And, if you feel sick, don't be afraid to abort the entry. No one is going to criticize you. Now, drink up and hit the road. I'm tired and we have a big day tomorrow."

They left, and I briefly went back to my past, back to the Navy for a yet another brush with history.

******

I was back on assignment to the *USS Yacht Sequoia*. Simple thing, yet, for a person who enjoys history, pretty thrilling. Was being on President Eisenhower's boat crew when he was at the war college in Newport yet another act of fate? Was it being in the right place at the right time? Or the wrong place at the wrong time? Guess it depends on how you view it. I have a pocket watch with the presidential seal on the face and Eisenhower's bust on the back from that assignment. That was a nice gesture on his part. It would seem this abused and neglected kid was certainly being exposed to some important people, and beginning to live an active role in some of this country's vivid history.

******

We spent the next week in training, learning to dress properly, donning safety equipment, wearing face masks.[xi] We were learning to read dosimeters,[xii] watching film, and getting familiar with the layout of the plant. Some guys failed the 100-question Radiation Work Permit (RWP) test we took late in the week; it was pretty tough. I suspect some failed on purpose as they did not seem to want to be here after they saw what was coming. Most of the guys from my outfit made it through, though.

The island was big, and somewhat intimidating. There was still a flurry of high brass on the site. The place was thick with NRC people and higher-ups from Babcock & Wilcox. Scientists were flown in from all over the world. It would seem the nuclear industry, as a whole, wanted to help prevent this event from snowballing. They didn't want the black eye. The industry claimed the plant was extremely safe, posing no more of a threat than coal-fired plants; they claimed nuclear fuel to be 100 times cleaner than coal. Still, this was big news. Cadres of media stayed to cover the story. I wonder if they knew what we know now, what I know now, would they still have hung around?

You see, when you deal with radiation, there are a series of concerns, serious concerns. You can't see it, taste it, or smell it; but, your body can absorb it. The slightest mishap could be life-altering. Was a subconscious deep-seeded fear beginning to play on my mind? Or was my guardian angel trying to tell me something? I shrugged it off, allowing my mind to wander back to a more pleasant life-altering experience.

******

It was August. I was home on leave. A friend was driving me home through town after a ball game. Once again, either fate or my guardian angel took control. I got out of the car while we waited at a red light. "Hey, where are you going?" my friend asked.

"Oh, I'm just going down the block for a few minutes. Pick me up?" I answered. When I tell you I had *no* reason to get out of that car, I mean I had *no* reason. Nor, did I have any reason to walk down the block. I cannot begin to explain why I did. Call it what you like, but that compulsion would convince me there was something greater in control...either fate or my guardian angel. Even to the present time, I have never figured out why I did what I did that afternoon. I had *no* reason to get out of that car. Or did I?

I found myself at the old J.J. Newbury store on Main Street in Stroudsburg. It was there that I was nearly run into by a girl pushing a baby in a stroller. I hadn't seen her coming from a side street. We excused each other; I watched as she walked away. She had shorts on and looked fantastic. I set on a bench and watched her as she continued walking down the street. Then, it hit me. That was *her*! That was Mary Ann; the girl of my dreams. The girl my friend had told me about right before I joined the Navy. I hollered her name and whistled at her. She turned around and walked back to me. We began to talk. Yes, she remembered me from the picture that ran in the paper when I joined the Navy. I asked her out, and the rest is history. We have been married 50 years.

How did that meeting come to be? What if I had not gotten out of the car? I like to think that even more than fate, my grandfather guided me to Mary Ann that day.

******

Monday morning. It was the first day of many days of entries into what we referred to as "no man's land." We met in the auditorium to familiarize ourselves with the Vi-Cam company personnel. They came from all over the country, but mostly the South. There were 3 offices, set up in trailers on the compound. We had about 25 men in ours, plus the Vi-Cam personnel and management (NRC, etc.).

We were from the Easton region, but there were men here from York, Lebanon, and Reading. There was even a small group here from a sub-district in Middletown. Most of the time we were split between other company people from these other districts; not all of the guys from the Easton region made their entries together. At the beginning, there were probably over 100 guys from companywide locations. Soon, however, with the conditions being as they were, the ranks began to thin.

Our foreman was a likable guy, bald; I teased him, calling him "Bullet Head." Well, he got even by sending me in more than once a tour when a single entry per day was the prescribed method. I asked him once what was going on. "Am I the only one here?"

"Wahoo," he said, "you're the only one I have faith in." I took that compliment with pride. Only, it put me in more risk-taking spots than most.

I made friends easily. Several of the men I befriended were permanent location people on the island, such as pump operators and mechanics. They would soon confide in me things that were going on unbeknownst to the public. Maybe these were just rumors, but they were interesting stories nonetheless. You know how those conversations go; they happen on a regular basis no matter what job you're working.

One night, back at the hotel, one of the guys came into my room. "Hey, Wahoo," he asked, "Do you have any pull with the cops down here?"

"No, can't say I do."

"Damn," he laughed, as he walked out the door. Guess he'd received a ticket for something or other. Sensing I was on the verge of another flashback, I thought to myself, *once a cop, always a cop.*

******

I joined the department in 1959. There were several reasons I had always wanted to become a policeman. Foremost, I suppose, was to elevate my social status, to distance myself from my lousy past and gain some respect. Just as importantly, though, I liked helping people. I enjoyed being able to do that as a cop.

I had a good understanding of the younger kids. I especially understood the ones who were borderline criminals; you know, the ones you knew were stealing, but you just couldn't prove it. Coming from the background I did, I had stolen things when I was young. When I was 14, I stole a pack of hot dogs from the supermarket. I was hungry; but, I wasn't too clever. As I walked through the parking lot, the manager called me back to the store and chewed me out. He demanded the package back. Then, he took my name and told me I had one hour to go to the police department to explain what I'd done. He said he was going to call to verify that I had done as I was told. Don't think that would be a tough punishment? Try it sometime.

59 long minutes later, I walked into the police department and spoke with the chief; the very same chief who would be my boss years later. I told him what I had done. He asked me if I had learned a lesson. "Yes, sir!" I replied. He then told me to go on home, adding that he would be watching me. Needless to say, I looked over my shoulder for quite some time after that.

That supermarket manager taught me a valuable life lesson; I wish I knew his name. Not only would I never steal again, but I had learned a technique that I would use quite often when I became a cop.

Whenever I stopped young, new drivers for an infraction, I would extend them the same deal that manager extended to me. I would take their information, complete with phone number. Then, I would tell them to go home and talk to their parents; I would be calling to find out if they had, indeed, done so. If they hadn't spoken to their parents, I would file the correct charges against their licenses for the infraction. You might be surprised just how long those young drivers would wait before talking to their parents. Then again, you might not. I would gauge the response from their parents when I called, deciding what they felt about the situation. Typically, I would then tell them to pull their child's license for a week, and forget about that first stop; but, I would be watching for future infractions.

Many years later, I would run into some of those same kids. They would remind me of our first meeting and tell me the encounter taught them a lesson; that always made me feel good. Some of the kids I've dealt with have told me they would have likely continued stealing and found themselves in jail had it not been for me. That kind of impact, to me, is what being a police officer is really about. Not all cops think that way. Some of the officers I worked with, in my opinion, should never have been given a badge. Notably, I found that to be the case with Marines turned cops. Their military training seemed to instill more of a "shoot-to-kill" than "subdue-and-restrain" approach; *aggressive* doesn't always get the job done best.

Don't get me wrong, certain aspects of the job do call for aggression; DUI crackdowns, for example. Regardless, I never believe a cop should just pull a weapon and shoot. Case in point. One night we had several officers chasing a teenager who was driving without a license. He was in a Volkswagen Beetle; you know, the type of car where the engine is literally in the trunk. What were the chances of a car like that speeding fast enough to outrun the police cruiser chasing it? The teenager was just scared and, so, was refusing to stop. One of the cops in the cruiser was gun-happy; he pulled out his 357-revolver and shot into the back of the car. It was a good thing the bullet hit the engine. That car remained under canvass for the better part of a year while the borough settled the case; there was no reason to draw a gun, never mind shoot.

You see all levels of society as a policeman – the good, the bad, and the real underbelly. You need to exercise good judgment.

******

A few weeks before Christmas, I was directing traffic so the local fire department could hang holiday decorations over the street. We had traffic down to one lane; I remember stopping one side, waving the other side through. I turned to the driver, motioning her to come ahead; she just shook her head and pointed. It took a few seconds to realize where she was trying to draw my attention. Those few seconds were all I had. I stepped back just in time; a car from the other lane was coming straight at me. My left hand caught his mirror, literally ripping it from the car. The driver had to stop as he could not get by the other car. I approached to chew him out, but was momentarily speechless as he looked at me and asked, "What's the matter, officer?" He spoke with slurred speech, of course.

After getting that driver out of the car, I gave him a quick sobriety test and called for back-up. In those days, it was standard procedure to take a person suspected of drunk driving to a doctor. Yes, it was still just "drunk driving" in those days; the term DUI had yet to be coined. When we finally found a doctor on call, we escorted the driver into his office.

All the while, this driver, who happened to be of some political importance in the county, kept telling me he would have my badge. He insisted he had only one drink before leaving his place of business. I had heard this line so many times; it was easy to ignore. Finally, after the doctor had examined the driver, I set him down in the waiting room. Before I went to confer with the doctor, I noticed a little pug-nosed dog running around in the corner. When I returned to escort the driver to the county jail, the dog was on his lap, licking his chin. Looking up at me, he said, "I'm going to sue you and have your badge. This won't hold up in court. You can't have me examined by no…Veterinarian!" Again, the line was delivered in a distinctively slurred voice. Well, that just made my day.

Later, some of his political friends tried to convince me to lessen the charges; I refused. I told one fellow he was no different or better than my illiterate aunt and her son; I'd already put them in jail for the same offense. As he hung up, I could hear him mumbling about what a nasty cop I was.

******

The worst calls a police officer can ever be summoned to are the domestic types; these always become the most violent. I remember one call I responded to; when I arrived, I found a husband straddling his wife, beating her face. I could clearly see she was pregnant, *very* pregnant. I grabbed his arm and ordered him to get off of her. Instead, he tried to hit me in the privates. I hit him across the shoulder blade with my night stick; this tactic usually numbs the arms to the point they won't move very well. Howling in pain, he rolled off her. What happened next? Well, that was the wife's cue to get up and start beating against my chest, yelling at me for hurting her husband. Go figure. I wound up arresting them both.

******

I had worked the midnight shift with the senior officer for about 3 years now. He was quite a character; later, he'd be promoted to chief. I was with him early one Saturday morning, patrolling near the bridge that connects the towns of Stroudsburg and East Stroudsburg. It was drizzling, a real nasty morning. It was then we came upon a car with New Jersey license plates; it was going the wrong way across the bridge. We had every intention of simply pulling up alongside the car to direct the driver to the correct side of the road, and then to send him on his way. But, just as we began to approach, the driver decided to take off at full speed.

My partner turned our vehicle around to pursue the car; I called in the description and the plates to the control center. I always had the habit of writing down the plate numbers. Before I could even ask, it was too late to seek assistance from the Stroudsburg department. We had been doing 80 miles per hour through the streets of Stroudsburg and had already reached State Highway 209. That route would lead us west out of town, where the road would become a twisted two-lane affair.

The control center called back to alert us the vehicle was stolen; we were to assume the occupants were armed. They had apparently pistol-whipped an elderly couple in a "Mom & Pop" store in Jersey.

We were hitting speeds of 90 to 100 miles per hour, lights on, siren blaring. My partner was a hell of an expert driver, keeping us within two car-lengths at all times; but, he was also a little bit crazy. He told me to fire a shot into the air. "Are you nuts?" I said. "We have the red light on, the siren going full blast, and you want me to shoot a shot in the air? No way." His next request was that I shoot out a tire. Now, I was a natural shot with a pistol; I had no reason to doubt I wouldn't miss my mark. I just had to question his logic. Think about it. Amidst all the excitement, and traveling at such high speed, your heart is pumping adrenalin furiously through your blood stream; every nerve in your body is alive with excitement. You really have to work to keep control of your senses. "Hell, with this mist?" I replied. "I can't even see a tire, let alone shoot it."

Suddenly, there was a flash of light from the suspects' car. My partner claimed they were shooting at us, but I wasn't exactly sure about that. He was, and it made him back off some. "What do you think, Richard?" he asked.

"Well, two things. Run them 'til they either run out of gas, or we do. And, meanwhile, I'll have the control center call the Fern Ridge State Police barracks for assistance." With that, there was another flash of light from the back of that car.

"You know they could kill someone before they run out of gas. The way they're driving? They just missed a car a few miles back."

"Okay, you convinced me," I conceded. "Get a little closer if you can." The car was a 1962 Ford with the gas refill behind the license plate. I told him I was sure I could hit it clean, but I'd rather skip a shot beneath it and hope it would just rupture the tank. "Or, I could put one through the back window."

"Well, do what you can."

Damn, I thought to myself, cowboys and Indians or G-men and robbers, take your pick. I now began to feel I was in the middle of one of the many movies I'd seen through the years. I rolled down the window, pulling my service revolver from the holster. I leaned out of the window, sure I did not want to hit the tank directly; a shot like that would cause the car to blow. So, I aimed right above the license plate, figuring, by our speed and distance, the bullet would drop down onto the road and skip into the tank. Holding steady as I could, squinting through the rain drops, I took aim and fired. The shot did exactly as I had hoped it would; one shot was all it took for the tank to spew gas all over our windshield. Pure luck? Or, was my grandfather there by my side, steadying my hand?

"Now, cowboy," I said, "back off and we'll follow until they run out of fuel."

"Hell of a nice shot!" he exclaimed.

"Pure luck," I replied. Luck wasn't on their side, though; a minute later, they missed a sharp turn in the road. The car crashed into the woods. I noticed their overhead light come on as both doors flew open. Into a very wet ditch, I stepped out of the cruiser. We could see them, but they would have a hard time seeing us without our lights on. One suspect took off up the road, my partner chasing him. The other stood by the open car door, holding something in his hand. I couldn't be sure what he was holding, but I was taking no chances. I had my revolver drawn. Aiming at him, I ordered him to put his hands in the air and walk towards me. He hesitated. "Look punk, I'm the guy that shot your gas tank," I said. "Do you think for one minute I could miss you at *this* range? Don't be stupid." With that, he raised his hands and began to walk toward me as instructed. Just then, a third man emerged from the car. I immediately shot into the ground to get his attention; that scared the both of them. The third suspect followed his pal, walking slowly towards me, hands in the air.

Another state police cruiser drove toward me as I handcuffed my suspects. My partner was in the back with the one he had taken off chasing; they'd been picked up about a mile down the road. As I put the two I had in the back seat, another state police cruiser arrived; we asked him to stay at the crash site until a tow truck could get to the car. We hauled our suspects to the county jail. Guess what? Turned out they were all juveniles, all under the age of 16. They thought this was "fun."

Those teenagers had not been shooting at us from that car; my partner had been wrong. They were using a flashlight to make us *think* they were; pretending, if you will, so they might scare us. Just goes to show, we weren't dealing with the sharpest criminal minds here; also goes to show, misinformation or misinterpretation of circumstances could be costly in our line of work. I would be remiss if I did not tell you that I often think of this incident, of how close I came to shooting a *mere* boy. Had I taken that shot, I undoubtedly would have killed him.

Ironically, I was the one who seemed to learn the valuable lesson that day. In the heat of the chase, there were so many emotions at play; there always are. You had to work to control those emotions, to do your job as an officer and keep everyone safe; you had to control your aggression at all times. Too many cops fall victim to what I like to call "Hero Syndrome," wanting to be thought of as a hero for capturing criminals, no matter the cost. These cops don't stop to think; they throw caution to the wind and ignore

42

all textbook procedures. All too often these rogue cops exacerbate dangerous situations leading to the death or injury of their fellow officers. They pull their guns for show of force, only to get themselves killed. You know the ones I'm talking about, you hear about them in the news all the time. That was not me; that was not why I became a police officer. I resigned from the department after that incident.

******

Yes, my experience as a police officer taught me many things; mostly, about the workings of society. No matter how right you are, someone will always tell you that you are wrong. Very few people will ever defend you, or pat you on the back to congratulate you for a job well done. Being a police officer is not what it is cracked up to be; you are damned if you do, and damned if you don't. You are the dividing line between law and violence.

The police department was quite an experience for me, back in the days of backyard justice, prior to the establishment of Miranda. Criminal suspects had no so-called "rights"; you could scare a few straight here and there. Now, was this all correct? Maybe it's like spanking your child; acceptable in my day, but not by a long shot in today's society. The justice system has effectively tied the hands of today's policemen, especially when it comes to the small, constant offenders. They get the standard slap on the wrist, followed by the warning not to do whatever they'd done again; but, sooner or later, they do it again. In my day, you took them out to the shed; they *didn't* do it again. There was a very fine line we walked as policemen. And, to be good policemen, sometimes that line had to be *properly* crossed.

******

Before I left the department, I happened upon a fellow we all knew was a thief. He was the type we could never seem to catch red-handed or come up with enough evidence against to make the arrest. I noticed his vehicle late one evening and pulled him over just to see what he was doing that time of night. Now, in today's world, this would be a definite "no-no"; it would be considered profiling. But, in my day, if it quacked like a duck, and walked like a duck, well, damn, if it wasn't a duck. I pulled him over.

The man was belligerent and defensive, wanting to know why I had stopped him. "Oh, just thought we could chat a bit," I said, casually.

"You know I don't like you, copper. We have nothing to chat about," he responded.

"Oh, I don't know about that. How come your license plate is so muddy?"

"How would I know? Look at the car. It needs to be washed," he growled.

"Yes, it does. But, this is your mother's car." I had seen the registration. "If you were a good son, you would wash it for her."

"That's none of your business, Pig."

Now, I usually didn't concern myself with someone calling me names; that goes with the job. But, since I was leaving the job, I thought this boy was due a little backyard justice. So, I shook his car down. There were a lot of hub caps in the trunk, from all sorts of cars. They were probably stolen, but, again, I couldn't prove it. "Where did all these come from?"

He replied in a snooty tone, "I stole them, copper. Now, try to prove it."

He was ticked off, to say the least. Tough. I made him take out the spare tire. He pulled it out, throwing it on the road such that it bounced back up to hit me in the shin. Now, that was the "no-no." I locked his car, made him pick up that tire, and told him to get in front of my police car. I got in, turned on the red light, and put the loud speaker outside so he could hear me. "Okay, smart guy," I said, "start heading for the inter-borough bridge. And, if you stop, or drop that tire, I will run you over in a heartbeat."

He responded, "You can't do this!" Guess what? I did.

Halfway down the road, he stopped. As promised, I nudged him with the front bumper. "What did I tell you?"

"It's too heavy," he moaned.

"Then start rolling it."

He started rolling the tire toward the bridge. When he finally crossed into the next town, I radioed one of their patrol cars. I knew all the men on duty. I told them I saw a suspicious man rolling a tire down from the bridge; they should probably check him out. The tire may be stolen. Well, they drove up to that poor, tuckered-out man rolling the tire (his tire); they recognized him, and knew about his elusive history. When they questioned him, he insisted it was his tire and told them what I had done. So, they called me to confirm his story. I said I knew nothing about it, reminding them how much that suspect liked to lie. Well, my fellow officers locked that man up for stealing a tire. When I got him out the next day, he apologized for mouthing off. Sometimes, you just need to have some backyard justice.

******

As we approached the road leading into the park, my partner said, "Richard, go into the park. We're going to save the county money."

"We are?" I replied. "How?"

"We're going to shoot this no-good bastard and throw his body in the river."

Several years back, my partner had been chasing a suspect down an alley. The suspect wouldn't stop running; so, my partner fired a shot into the air to startle him. By accident, he blew out a street light. He never did catch the suspect that day; but, he vowed he would get him some day down the line. Lo and behold, that day had arrived. A woman swore out a warrant against her live-in boyfriend. The Justice of the Peace called us to execute the warrant. Well, guess who it was? My partner was tickled to no end; said he was "finally going to get that bastard." So, we waited until about two o'clock in the morning, figuring he would show up at his girls' place. Sure enough, he did, and we caught him.

I was driving; my partner was in the passenger seat, suspect in the back. We were heading to the county jail, but not directly; first, we would have to pass the local park. My partner was ready for some backyard justice of his own, asking me to pull into the park so he could just shoot the bastard. The suspect began hollering, begging me not to listen to my partner. As we approached the park, he began screaming even louder, beginning to call me names. All the while, my partner was aggravating the suspect, insisting he was going to shoot him. Finally, I decided to go along with it; I pulled into a secluded part of the park. I got out, opened the back door, and said, "Get out. I don't want any blood in the back of this car." As I reached in to grab him, the guy tried to bolt past me. He knocked off my hat, and was just about to throw a punch. Just then, a shot rang out. I must have jumped two straight feet up in the air. That knuckle-headed partner of mine had just fired a shot into the ground behind me; I thought for sure my partner had shot him. The suspect was so scared that he fainted, falling flat on the ground.

"Okay," I said to my partner. "You had your fun. Now, you put him in the car and take him to jail. I'm walking back to the station." As I started to walk away, he was shoving the suspect into the back seat; he was laughing the entire time. The next day, as I escorted that suspect to his hearing, all the while he continued to tell me he was nothing short of being very sorry for his actions.

******

It was a very cold, snowy Saturday night, late in the month of December, just before the Christmas holiday. I was working alone, doing something I enjoyed. I was walking the beat. A tall man approached me; he had a weather-beaten face and carried a worn old bag. "Sir," he said. "Could you tell me where a Salvation Army shelter might be?"

"Sorry," I replied, "but, there are none in the area."

His shoulders sank as he hunched up and continued to walk along the darkening street. I turned, calling him back. "Where are you headed?" He told me he was going to the

48

Shawnee Inn in hopes he might see Fred Waring;[xiii] he knew him personally. The man thought maybe Mr. Waring could help him get a job as a dishwasher.

I guess there was just something about the man. Or, perhaps, thinking back, my grandfather was operating again? It was just so bitter cold. Even a dog, like the one who shared her house and kept me warm that night so long ago, should have shelter on a night like this.

We had two holding cells at the police station that were usually kept very warm; we used those particular cells to dry out the drunks. I told the man, if he didn't mind spending the night in a cell, he was welcome to the shelter. I would arrange for him to stay the night; I would leave the cell door open. He was so grateful. I walked him to the station and got him settled before I headed home for dinner.

Mary Ann and I lived in an apartment just a block from the station. We did not have much, but the wife was, is, a fine cook. Tonight it was meatloaf, potatoes, and corn. I told her about the fellow, suggesting we might prepare him a platter. She agreed; so, I took dinner and a thermos of coffee back to him. He had tears in his eyes when I gave him the meal; he thanked me profusely.

Later, as I sat in the office, reading the paper, he walked out of the holding cell with a battered old instrument case he'd taken from his bag. He opened the case; it was a trumpet, shiny and well-cared for. He asked if he could play something for me. "Sure, why not?" He played the sweetest song; I was impressed. Then he said, "Tommy Tucker. I played for my supper." I just laughed.

After I dropped that fellow off at the Shawnee Inn the next morning, I didn't think anything further of our meeting. About a year later, I received a card in the mail. It was from his daughter, postmarked from somewhere upstate New York. She thanked me for being so kind to her father. It was by that letter I learned the man had once played in Fred Waring's band. So, I thought, that was the connection! The letter went on to explain how very difficult it had been for her father to play for me; he was suffering from throat cancer, dying. I never forgot that letter, and I will never forget that man. I wish I had kept it.

I never thought about that relatively small event as being one that could hold such great meaning, but now, as I look back, it was one of those few rewarding moments for being a cop. I was able to help someone, to keep someone safe, and that made me feel great about being a policeman. Yet, again, I am left to question whether my encounter with this man had been fate, or had it been something greater. Was I put there in that particular place, at that particular time, for a particular reason?

******

The doorway was tented; several large fans were blowing into the building, stirring the dust inside. Dust, mind you, that was radioactive. How would we begin to tackle such an enormous undertaking? The time had approached for our first foray into the aux building. It was the first time we were actually seeing just what was in store for us on this island.

"Remember," the health physic (HP) warned, "don't take your mask off. If possible, get to the door first." Our four-man team was ready to enter. Our foreman was Vi-Cam; these guys were known in the industry as "Generation Jumpers." They were constantly used until they reached the maximum dosage for allowed radiation exposure, then, they were shipped out; the yearly allotment was 5000 milirems,[xiv] 1250 a quarter.

That first entry was a learning experience. We made our way through a maze of tools and equipment, struggling to breathe through the masks; one big fellow from the York district seemed to be having particular trouble. Couple difficult breathing with the fear of the unknown in this type of deadly atmosphere, and I don't care what you may *think*, you find out just how big and tough you *really* are. The fear of the unknown works on your mind and your body, raising your heart rate and blood pressure. Even though it was worse for the guys new to this line of work, no amount of training could have completely prepared any of us for work under these conditions. Call it pride, or bull-headedness, whichever, we toughed it out. Like most men, we didn't want to fail in the eyes of our peers.

Once we were acclimated to the conditions, the job was relatively simple; but, acclimating to those conditions was *far* from simple. We had to climb a flight of stairs to the 2nd floor, hauling some work tools back down to be bagged. The climb was hard on the lungs; we could hardly see through the small face plates in those masks. By the time we reached the top of the stairs, we were all straining to breath. Imagine trying to hold your breath as long as you could while swimming underwater; that was what it felt like. The fellow from York never did make it to the 2nd floor; halfway up, he fell to his knees and sprawled out. I tried to get him to a sitting position to regain control, telling him to sit and bend forward. He couldn't catch his breath. Now, he was no small man; he had to weigh well over 200 lbs. before he put all on all that heavy protective gear. I was concerned he might begin to hyperventilate, but I had to be careful not to compromise his suit. He was mumbling something I couldn't understand through his mask. The other guys thought he was just taking a break and pressed ahead to the landing, but I thought maybe he was having a heart attack.

Bending into his face, I could hear him more clearly. "Take me out, please, I can't breathe." His face plate was clouded, his head in his hands; he was trembling like a leaf in a windstorm. The other guys, having no idea what was going on, only waved back to me when I waved for their attention. Thinking maybe they would follow if I started down the stairs with him, I decided I couldn't wait any longer to get this fellow out of the building. Now, I'm not exactly a small man, but it was a strain to lift him to his feet. My heart was racing. "Jack!" I kept calling his name. "Get it together and stand up. Hold onto me. I'll get you to the door." He mumbled something; I think it was "Okay, Wahoo."

I managed to get him to the clean entry area, dragging and pulling him along the way. Thankfully, it wasn't terribly far. I motioned to the HP, who knew instantly there was a problem. He helped me get Jack near a fan and removed his mask. Jack sucked in the fresh air; his face was contorted and reddish-purple. I moved back into the building and began to peel off my own gear, stepping on each clean area pad until I was down to my underwear. I was drenched in sweat from the excitement.

When we got back to the trailer later that afternoon, the big fellow from York thanked me. He left; he would never come back. As I showered that night, the water beating down on me, my mind once again took me back a few years.

******

The spray of salt water stung as it hit my face. The waves were coming over the bow of the ship; one minute we were on top of a mountain, the next we were deep down in a valley. I felt like I was on a roller coaster. We were in the middle of a violent hurricane, in the middle of the Bermuda Triangle.

My ship, the *USS Yosemite AD19*, was the flag ship of the 6th destroyer fleet. We had just left Cuba en route to Bermuda. Having the flag admiral aboard warranted a squadron of destroyers as an escort, but they were nowhere in sight. In fact, I couldn't see anything except water, in any direction...including up; it was so dark the sky even looked like water. The ship was over 500 feet long and 75 feet wide, crewed by close to 1000 men; it was not a small ship (*see illustrations*). Right now, though, we were being tossed around so violently that you'd think it was a cork in a bathtub.

Every three minutes, the quarterdeck would announce, "Starboard side awash, port side[xv] lee. All hands remain below decks!" The water came down starboard with such force; it was like a dam had given way somewhere. The scuppers couldn't handle it fast enough to get off the deck. The bow shuddered as it climbed the enormous waves, only to slide back down the other side. Every time the stern came out of the water, the screws would shake the ship; it vibrated like a runaway washing machine. The expansion plates were slamming as if being struck by a tremendous sledge hammer. Wave after wave hit the bow; each time, the ship would almost stand still as it strained to remain on course. Several waves hit us on a quarter, rolling the ship over until the yardarms looked like they were going to hit the sea. The two helmsmen on the quarterdeck wheel fought to keep the bow steered into the giant waves. If a wave hit from the side, we would roll over like a dead fish.

Below decks there was nothing to be done. Young guys were crying; some were throwing up. We had to strap ourselves to our racks[xvi] if we wanted to lie down without falling out. As you would expect, no one was worrying about eating. I could actually feel the blood flowing from my head to my feet. Our ship took that beating for many long hours, but, at the time, I had no idea just how bad things really were above deck.

My quarters were one deck below the boat deck aft. The chief quartermaster on the bridge sent a messenger down; the captain wanted to know if we could unbutton the port side boat crane to swing the boom out. We kept yawing to starboard. Since the big cranes were aft, he must have had something in mind. Or, was he readying us to abandon ship? "This is kind of crazy, don't you think?" I said to the chief. He just shrugged his shoulders, closing his eyes. I went on, "Chief, you do know I have to free-hand climb that crane, which is tricky enough while we are tied to a pier…let alone under these conditions?"

"You can do it, boy. I know you can," he replied.

"Yeah, but if I slip, no one will ever find me. I'll be chewed up by the propellers."

"Well," he laughed, "then don't slip."

Since I was also a boat coxswain, my job, if the captain had decided to abandon ship, would have been to get as many small boats into the water as I could, starting with the admiral's barge and followed by the rest of the motor launches. The last one would be for me and my crew; that is, if there was time for a last one. I knew there wouldn't be; I would never get off that crane alive.

******

Will we get off this island alive? That was the question of the hour as I sat chewing the fat with a couple of the guys. There was so much radioactive debris in that building; it seemed it would take forever to clear the proper avenues to proceed further, let alone to make it into the containment building. The company seemed to think we could get Unit 2 back in service within a couple of months; I had my doubts. Rumors continued to circulate about the safety of the plant as a whole. Was the reactor really in a stable condition? Just how much radiation were we being exposed to?

******

Off the island, our private lives were "disrupted," to say the least. Some of the guys really partied with the southern boys while they were away from their spouses; things could get pretty wild. Lou was on an all-out hunt for a new woman. Well, he found her, and fell head-over-heels in love with her. Lou was always "in love" with a strange skirt, but this one was serious. Now, I told you before that Lou and Tony would have a confrontation; this was it. Apparently Tony had already taken this same woman to bed. Tony really began to rub Lou on a daily basis, telling him how good she was in the sack. The tension between them bled right over into the job.

Both Lou and Tony were with me on a routine entry one day. The job today was to hose down some zoomies.[xvii] This was usually just a hose-and-contain until we could either gather the residue and bag it, or send it down to the sump pump. There was nothing too bad or dangerous about the task, unless, of course, you got careless. I was getting a drum ready to insert a special bag; Lou was handling a small hydrolyser.[xviii] Tony, well, Tony proceeded to write on a small piece of cardboard about an obscene act he'd performed with Lou's new girlfriend. Next thing I knew, Lou was blasting Tony with the hydrolyser, an instrument that was powerful enough to tear paper or plastic right in half; if Lou kept blasting, he could compromise Tony's safety gear. Tony couldn't reach Lou, but, had he been able to, there would have been hell to pay. Tony was about 5'9" to Lou's 6'3", but he was more than a little stressed-out; they both were. If they began to throw punches, their charcoal cartridges could be compromised or their masks pulled off, risking serious exposure.

In all the years I had worked for the company, I had never witnessed, nor even heard of, any fights on company property. Now, here, these two are fighting like they're in some back alley instead of a high-risk atmosphere; this was not good, to say the least. Not only were they risking their lives, but if they continued their behavior, the entry would surely be reviewed. We would all end up on the carpet,[xix] and our RWP's would be terminated.

I stepped in between them, pulling them apart. My back was to Lou, as I knew he'd know better than to tangle with me as I calmed Tony down. I told Lou to go to the first step-off pad[xx] to undress and leave; I then admonished Tony, who immediately apologized, and told him to help me finish the job. Later, standing in our skivvies in the dressing room, I told them both, in no uncertain terms, to take their beef off the island; I would cover it up this once, but "you can bet you won't be making any more entries with me...at least, not the two of you, together." The tension between them would not have been conducive to teamwork.

Such was the internal stress on the island, albeit self-inflicted. Lou ended up making more entries with other teams, and, eventually, he became a de-con foreman. Go figure. I don't know for sure if the tension between them ever came to blows again; they avoided each other as much as possible, both on and off the island. Tony and I spent a lot of time together at Hershey Bears' hockey games; we would hit different bars for dinner or a nightcap. On several occasions, we ran into Lou and that girl of his; she would always manage to wind up somewhere near Tony, only deepening their rift. Lou eventually divorced his wife, leaving him free to marry that woman who made their emotions run so hot that day. Tony found himself a real nice girl of his own to marry some years later.

******

Rumors on the island ran rampant among the locals. Something was always being said about those who chose not to evacuate during the incident. Some people claimed they were coming down with mysterious illnesses. Others claimed their animals were acting strangely; one fellow even said his chickens were laying odd-colored eggs. Seemed funny to me, but I supposed there would be many such stories in the days ahead. These rumors would eventually make the journey straight into folklore.

******

I've always had big shoulders, the welcoming, strong shoulders that encourage people to confide in me. Such was the case with my friend, Jim. He had been staying in his fifth wheel trailer at a local campground instead of lodging at the motel; a month before my second trip down, he asked me if I'd like to share the rent on the next go-around. Jim was going through some marital problems at the time, so the companionship would do him good. Funny, it seemed I was always with the guys who had marital problems. Maybe they looked to me as a voice of stability.

Monday morning. Instead of entering the main gate to the plant as usual, Jim and I were redirected to the back gate because of some protest activity. "Hell of a sight," I thought aloud as I was now viewing those huge hyperbolic-shaped towers from a different vantage point. As we walked to the inner gate that would lead us into the compound, we noticed security had been tightened. There was a big black fellow, an ex-football player, doing pat-downs. I thought I might joke with him a little that morning, lighten the mood. "Wahoo, take off your hat," he instructed, as everyone was to remove their hard hats for inspection.

"I can't, Sam," I responded, to his surprise. When he asked why not, I said, "I have a grenade under it."

Well, you can imagine that didn't go over so well. He gave me holy hell, pulling me from the line. After some jaw-boning, and after everyone else had cleared the security checkpoint, he finally let me go through. I imagine everyone was on edge because of the protest at the main gate that morning. Still, I didn't play those games anymore.

We were briefed on the elevator entry when we got to our trailer. The HP's had made an earlier entry with Geiger counters and had discovered the pit had radioactive readings up to 5000 milirems; that wasn't only considered *very high,* that just about capped a year's dosage allotment to a nuke worker. The radiation was migrating up the shaft, indicated by the escalating reading on the 2nd floor. As long as the doors were kept closed and sealed, it would be possible to contain the "hot spot"; but, this would be tricky. When the elevator had to be put into operation and brought down, which was necessary to de-con the 2nd floor, the building was flooded with nuclear wastewater, creating a wonderland of contamination; workers' tools and materials were now highly radioactive.

The lights set up by the previous teams cast an eerie glow through the wood scaffolding and into the confines; it was kind of spooky. The porous cement had soaked up the radiated water; there were small pockets of wet glaze on the walls and in the corners. The floor was definitely "hot," but, if we could seal this highest source of radiation, another team could follow us in to seal off the walls.

I was assigned to work with Jim, and I had a lot of faith in him; he was a bull. We had to work fast to ensure minimal exposure, but we had to perform each task slowly and deliberately so we didn't compromise our safety suits. Teams had been sent in prior to ours to clear and neutralize the area. Jim and I were paired with two guys from another district as the elevator team. Isolating the source of radiation here would be difficult because of the weight of the lead blankets; as if getting those blankets into position wasn't bad enough under simple circumstances, wrestling them down into the elevator shaft amidst all the radiation in the pit presented an even greater challenge.

We jumped the 4 feet into the pit, then, proceeded to lay out the 60-pound lead blankets. The blankets were not only bulky and awkward, but they had to be handled with extreme caution to avoid compromising our protective gear. We could use nothing but the strength in our hands and arms; we could not afford to risk bringing the blankets into our bodies for leverage; their edges were rough and could rip through our suits. Cautious of our gloves, we worked to spread those blankets across the floor of wet, highly-contaminated cement. The extreme heat built up in our suits, as our lungs continued to labor through the particulate masks. Those masks allowed only about 80 percent oxygen into our lungs, and, as we expended air, the small face plates in those masks would fog, dimming our sight. Trying to stay calm under these conditions, while intent on completing the job as quickly and efficiently as possible, only quickened our heart rates.

I don't recall exactly how long it took to cover that entire floor, but we were drenched in sweat. I boosted Jim out of the pit; he, in turn, grabbed my hands and pulled me out. We undressed at each step-off pad until we were down to our shorts. It felt so good to finally remove that mask and take in a really deep breath of clean, fresh air. When we got back to our trailer, the foreman told us we had done "a fine job"; that was the only "hot job" Jim and I performed together on the island. Later, we found ourselves assigned to separate shifts.

* * * * * *

It was noon, but damned if I didn't find myself hungry or thirsty after the morning's entry; didn't stop me from downing a big glass of ice tea while kibitzing with the other guys. It was just then we heard the klaxon go off, signaling a shutdown. The island was being buttoned-up; everyone was ordered to remain where they were. "Can't be Unit 2," I said, to no one in particular. Unit 1 was still operating. Everyone just sat there in awe, looking at each other, wondering what the hell was going on. "Damn," I sighed to Jim, "I don't need any more excitement today." He nodded in agreement.

We had seen security vehicles driving down the road with their lights blazing, but it wasn't until we saw the state police car go by the window that we began to wonder how serious it really was; they don't just ride out to the island for nothing. It turned out to be two separate concerns, neither of which was as monumental as we feared. One, a small motor boat had come too close to the perimeter of the island; perceived as a possible security threat, it had to be investigated. Two, several hand guns were found in a pickup truck that had been stopped on the bridge; hence, the arrival of the state police. For the next several weeks, the guards would be checking every single vehicle, coming and going; in the days prior, they had just been doing spot checks, maybe every other vehicle. Security was tightening.

******

63

It would seem things off the island remained heated, too. The "no nukes" crowd, the same people who had blocked our entrance to the plant, seemed to have no other purpose in migrating to the island than to stir up bad sentiments. This crowd primarily consisted of outsiders, not locals. Most of the locals were savvy enough to know the reactor could not just spontaneously explode, that there were no elements in a nuclear reactor capable of causing an explosion. They knew a meltdown was the real danger; they knew the hydrogen bubble that formed during those long hours following the meltdown had posed its own unique threat of explosion. In light of that knowledge, most of the people who had lived here all their lives were back to a sense of normalcy, at relative ease, after the initial incident.

******

After working a 3 to 11 shift one night, Jim and I decided to stop to unwind on the way back to the trailer. We pulled into a local bar, got a beer and began to shoot pool. There was one little old lady who looked to be about 60 sitting at the end of the bar; the bartender was young, probably about 30. It was quiet. After about an hour, four young guys came in wanting some beer; they looked like they had already had one too many. I believe the bartender may have known them; he told them to go home. These wise guys were pretty unhappy with his suggestion. One of them picked up a chair and threw it at the old lady at the end of the bar, knocking her straight to

64

the floor. With that, the bartender leaped over the bar and took two of them down. The other two started back towards him. The one closest to me looked like he might have a knife in his hand; I didn't take the time to make sure. Being an ex-police officer, I had been in these types of situations before; if he had a knife, he would assume I was scared of him. The only thing to do was meet him head on, negating his advantage.   So, my pool stick became a night stick. I jammed the butt end into his stomach.   He let out some cry as he doubled over, coughing and spitting. Breaking the stick over his back, I knocked him to the floor, where he lay in a fetal position. The old lady was cursing and shouting, so, I figured she wasn't hurt. I motioned Jim to the side door, thinking we didn't need to be there when the police arrived. Needless to say, we didn't do much unwinding that night...and, we never returned to that bar.

******

The reactor on Three Mile Island is a pressurized water reactor (PWR). These reactors are designed like thermal reactors, requiring the fast fusion[xxi] neutrons to be slowed down in a process called moderation, or thermalization, in order to interact with the nuclear fuel to sustain a chain reaction. To maintain primary system temperature at the desired point, boron is used as a moderator. As in most commercial PWRs, varying concentrations of boric acid allows for the reactivity adjustment in the control rods to be sustained at 100% power as the fuel is burned up.

******

It was extremely hot inside that relatively small room, very hard to breath; the water had raised the humidity to a saturation point where the walls and ceiling were as wet as the floor. I felt like I was in a jungle gym as I worked to dodge the big valves, tanks, and all that piping. It was very hard to see anything through the small, foggy window of my face mask, let alone the spread of radiated water. I was only aware of what was in my immediate view; I was trying to keep the water away and the zoomies at bay, concentrating on the boron. I should have known by now that nothing would ever be simple here.

I had been assigned to make entry with a fellow from the Lebanon district. I told him to stand to my left and use the squeegee to push the water toward the drain while I handled the hose. Shortly after making entry, I felt a hand on my shoulder; in less than a second that same hand began to slip away. The squeegee lay flat at my feet. Hearing a gurgled "Wahoo," I turned to find the young lad on his knees, trying to get off the floor. He was in distress. The floor was wet and slippery; he wasn't getting up. I must admit, I wasn't sure what had happened; but, I was now between a rock and a hard place. We had not had any training to assimilate such an event as this. We were told we could tear off our masks if absolutely necessary, but no one I knew would take that option seriously. No one in their right mind, at least. To be "crapped up"[xxii] on

66

the skin was one thing, but to inhale or ingest the radiated dust in the air was quite another.

The HPs could not see us; even if they had, they couldn't help, they weren't dressed out. I jammed the hose as far as I could down the open drain; I couldn't just drop it, nor could I turn with it in my hand. Once free of the hose, I leaned down and put my arms under his, lifting him to his feet. It was only then, face to face, that I could see his mask was full of vomit. He was choking, his eyes wide with fear.

Quickly, I pushed him to the door and out into the clean air. I ripped off his mask; at the same time, I was yelling at the top of my lungs for help. It took a few seconds for the HPs to react. Two of them dragged him out to the staging area, which was immediately cast into a state of confusion and medical reaction. There was nothing more I could do at that point. So, I went back in; with one hand on the squeegee and one directing the hose, I finished the job. After the last of the water was down the drain, I covered it and looked to make my way out. The HPs were in the process of cleaning up the area and putting down new pads. My first question to them was whether the young lad was alright; he was. We both came out "clean," the job was secure. It was an experience I never wanted to repeat.

When I got back to the trailer, that fellow from Lebanon was getting ready to go home. He thanked me profusely, all the while apologizing for the trouble. I told him it was no big deal, I was just glad he didn't get "crapped up," that he was okay. He never came back to the island. In fact, over the next few months, it seemed quite a few boys left, never to return.

******

The island was sometimes akin to a circus. Between the continuous stream of media and tour buses, it seemed the population on the island had tripled from when we first arrived. The Visitor's Center always seemed to be abuzz; some people were so peaked with curiosity they would peer through field glasses to get a better view. The local paper kept us all abreast of daily events on the island; there were parties almost every night. The bars must have done record business during that time. The atmosphere was just unreal.

What was even more unreal was the number of rumors, conspiracy theories, cover-up allegations, and "blame campaigns" that had begun to circulate. The movie *China Syndrome* had instigated several of these rumors, as the governor had feared would be the case from his first knowledge of the incident; but, nonetheless, these rumors crossed the lips of many. Was there a mole in the plant? Was there a saboteur? Some HPs fueled the rumor mill, alleging the released radiation was much greater than the NRC and the company had reported. Meanwhile, the company sought to blame the incident on Babcock &

Wilcox, who, in turn, blamed the company for poor personnel training; this was an argument that would go back and forth for years. As if all that tension wasn't enough, a power struggle continued between the nuclear industry and the NRC, their supposed "watchdog." Rumors prevailed that the NRC had turned a blind eye to the company, making allowances for shortcuts. Was it possible these supposed shortcuts led up to the incident?

With so much speculation, I have to assume no one will ever know the answers for sure. Most likely, as seems typical, the ones at the bottom of the heap will be the fall guys. Listening to all the rumors, I would just shake my head and think, "too much conjecture for me. I just follow orders."

******

"Damn, Chief, you need a straw to drink that coffee."

He laughed, "You are right, young man, you are right."

"So, are we still going to go through with this?"

"Son, you're in the Navy. Orders are orders."

Yeah, I thought, can't get around orders in the Navy; I was just hoping they may have changed their minds. Instead, the order stood. I buttoned my foul-weather jacket and opened the door. "Be right back, Chief. I have to call the engine room for power to the crane."

"Okay, son. I'll try to finish this coffee," he jested, as I slid and staggered to the mast that held the ship phone. Holding onto the mast, I picked up the receiver, punched in the number, and listened for the voice that would say "Engine Room."

"Yeah, this is Lesh on the boat deck. I need power to the port side crane."

"Power to the crane? Are you crazy?" he asked.

"Not me. But, maybe someone with more rank than I have might be. But, you know, come to think of it, you may be right, I might just have to be a little crazy. This isn't the brightest thing to do."

"Dick, you aren't going to climb up there are you?" I recognized the voice now; his name was Johnson. We had some liberty together; he lived in the Easton area of Pennsylvania, not far from my hometown.

"Looks that way, Johnny. Sure can't fly up there...but sure as hell can fly *off* there," I told him.

"Pal, you are one crazy man."

"Orders are orders, Johnny, so light it off."

"You got it, buddy. Be damned careful. And, by the way, can I have your car?" he chuckled.

Before I hung up, I replied, "Sure, pal." One thing was for sure. Someone was crazy. For a split second, I stopped to
70

wonder if I would live through this. Would I live to get married? To have grandkids? "Hell," I thought as I struggled to make it back to the deck house. Just climbing the ladder to get up here on the boat deck was a challenge, and that was only 8 feet high; I couldn't imagine what trouble it was going to be to climb that crane 40 feet from the bottom of the deck to the control platform...in the midst of hurricane-force winds. The laddered rungs were welded on the side, but there was no cage, nothing to keep me from rolling side to side or forward to aft in time with the movement of the ship...nothing except my hands and feet. I had climbed those rungs thousands of times without a single misstep, but never under these conditions. What a man wouldn't do for $60.00 a month!

******

We were making big bucks during those days in de-con. Off the island, everyone just let their hair down and ran wild; they were away from home with pockets full of cash. The campground was packed all week. One of the younger guys had also decided to lodge here instead of a motel. He parked his truck camper, a slide-in, in the lot next to ours. He propped the camper up on blocks and legs, then, slid out the truck so he could use it during the week. Something about the way he propped up that damn thing didn't look quite safe to me, but, he insisted it was fine, climbing the steps to prove it. The very next weekend, his young wife came down for a visit. Jim and I heard a crash about midnight; we heard laughter and went out to see what was going on. There was his camper, on the ground, fallen right off those blocks. It seemed he and his wife making violent love that night had proven too much for the unit. Now, I have seen those bumper stickers that read "Don't come a knockin' if this camper's a rockin'," but I will be damned if thought I'd ever see the result. I did that night. It took 10 of us to help him lift the unit back up on those blocks; then we chipped in and told him we'd rent them a hotel room for the night. His wife was one embarrassed lady. The guys busted him for some time after; they wouldn't let it rest. But, he was a good sport, just took it in stride.

******

Then there was the guy from up in Dingmans' Ferry. Boy, did we meet some characters. We called him "Dudley" because he was always at the butt of a joke. He must have been a guy who enjoyed pain; he would be 20 feet away from you, challenge you to a duel, then just smile and say he was kidding when you'd catch him. Some of the guys had a stick; they called it "The Dudley Stick," and would bang him with it. He'd whine, but he always came back for more.

Dudley was rooming with a couple of guys from Easton who could be quite cruel, carrying jokes a little too far. These guys knew Dudley suffered from hemorrhoids. Once, when he wasn't looking, they took his tube of cream and spiked it with Tabasco sauce. As if that wasn't bad enough, they switched the knobs on the shower. Well, poor old Dud, he fell for it; he used that cream and went ballistic, heading to the shower and turning that cold water tap. Sure enough, hot water hit his backside, sending him straight through the roof, naked as a jaybird.

Those roommates of his pulled a few other nonsensical pranks on him. They went so far as to paint the bottom of his shoes with luminescent paint, convincing him he was "crapped up." Dudley was so scared, he threw away his shoes. Funny thing, though; he seemed to enjoy the attention every time someone would tell one of those stories.

******

The Southern boys brought some character of their own to the island. The Vi-Cam outfit from Mississippi included a member of the Ku Klux Klan. Supposedly he was an exalted leader; he was known as "The Grand Imperial Wizard," though his real name was Doug. Rumor had it his room was decorated with all kinds of Klan paraphernalia and Rebel flags. Some of the Northern guys thought it would be fun to bust his butt a little, so, they got together and schemed.

They made a cross out of newspapers, and they borrowed some entry hoods from the site ("clean" hoods, of course). After turning out the lights, one guy went over to the Vi-Cam trailer and asked Doug to come over. As soon as he walked in the door, he saw all those Northern guys sitting

73

around a table in their hoods, watching that cross burn. He immediately laughed, offering to sign them all up! The levity was good for morale; it lessened the fear and the tension that came with the job.

******

Friday night, just before quitting time. Bullet Head, our foreman, called me over to tell me there had been a bad accident in the science lab; he needed a two-man crew. He asked me to stay. I agreed and headed for the "hot house" entrance as he instructed. As I dressed out alongside a fellow from York in the locker room, it was explained to us that a beaker of "highly-toxic contamination" had fallen on the floor when the tech left the lab. The fluid ran towards the drain, where it mixed with water; the reaction left the room filled with fumes from the emitted gas. The lab had to be secured. The doors were sealed; all possible cracks were sealed.

We doubled our rain suits and put on as many pairs of gloves are we could; the same with the booties.[xxiii] After we were completely dressed, a few guys helped us strap on our scuba gear and breathing masks, ensuring they were sealed to our faces. It had been at least 30 years since I'd dressed out in scuba gear, I thought, while they proceeded to tape our canvas hoods all around the perimeters. Then, they placed additional raincoat-type hoods over those, again sealing them with tape. We were taking every possible precaution. We were told it would be "okay" touching the fumes, but "deadly" breathing them. Nice.

As we approached the door, we plugged in our breathing hoses, turned on the tanks and tested our masks for leaks. Everything seemed to be in order. We wasted no time making the entry through the tent as the powerful fans behind us blew in fresh air to keep containment to the lab. Once we made entry, the doors were shut and resealed. We were essentially "locked in."

Our job was to remove the beaker and broken glass, flushing it down the drain with a neutralizer. The job was relatively simple on paper; the problem was the toxic atmosphere. If going into a radiation field was considered bad, going into a room filled with toxic gas was dire. We were told the job had to be done as soon as possible, all tracks covered. I took that sense of urgency and caution to mean they wanted to keep the NRC out of it; there were already so many investigations going on here.

My partner pushed the glass around as I carefully double-bagged what was left of the beaker. Without the water accelerant, the contents of the beaker were relatively harmless, but, we had to be careful not to cut our gloves on the broken glass; the air around us was already deadly. We scrubbed the outside of the drain with a cloth, poured down the neutralizer, and screwed in a cap. The time must have been going faster than I thought, because, just then, my partner's bell went off, indicating he had only about 2 minutes of air left in his tank. Maybe he was breathing faster than I was? In any event, we had yet to finish securing the drain. I took a deep breath, turned my tank off, and motioned for him to exit; I would finish alone. After sealing the drain with plastic, my lungs needed some air. I turned my tank back on; that air sure did taste good. Just as I affixed the last piece of tape to secure that plastic, my bell rang. The HP opened the door for me to exit into the path of that huge fan. Even though it only washed over the wet layer of protective gear, that blast of air felt good. I proceeded to the staging area to undress, peeling off layer by layer and bagging the whole unit. I thought a cold shower, followed by a cold beer, would feel good right about then.

Back at the trailer, Bullet Head filled out my overtime sheet. "Good job, Wahoo."

"Yeah," I replied, "another day, another dollar." I definitely earned that one. The next week Bullet Head let me slide a couple of days. "Nice guy," I thought.

******

As the months went on, the optimism that the job could be done to reopen the plant within a year had begun to fade. The political blame game was delaying our progress; the push to enter the sealed reactor room seemed to have been set aside. Our work force began to dwindle. The Southern Vi-Cam boys had reached their dosage quotas and were being sent home. The ones who were left on the island still had a lot of partying left in them. They drank this stuff called "white lightning" – potent; it was the worst stuff I ever tasted. Those boys could really play their guitars; even though the daily party scene was not my style, I occasionally joined them with my harmonica. They loved the New Orleans Blues I played on that harmonica, said it made me "one of them."

New teams had been sent in from other districts to replace those who had reached their quotas; they didn't cope well at all with the unknown when it came to their first entries. Many of them were immediately "crapped up" and, after a hard scrub-down, simply returned to their home stations, never to return. Some were unable to handle the feeling of claustrophobia that came from wearing the masks. Others were outright disenchanted and just left.

All the while, the media continued to play on the fears of the public, reminding them daily of the "worst nuclear accident on American soil." The public remained on edge. Even the locals had now begun to favor the "no nukes" sentiment.

Men were being shuffled from all over the company to take a tour as foremen on the island. I had worked with one such fellow as a first class lineman in the Easton district; he was now down here as our foreman. His name was Robert. He was a character, to say the least; a good guy, who wouldn't admit to it. We'd had our moments in the past, but we respected each other to get the job done right. He told me about a time he'd gone out for drinks with the Southern Vi-Cam foreman I introduced to you earlier, Doug, "The Grand Imperial Wizard of the Ku Klux Klan." They stopped at a little bar outside of town, "The Railroad House"; it seemed there were only four people in there that night, four men of color. Now, Doug was Jewish. So, you might think, having known his share of prejudice, he wouldn't be one to condone it; but it would soon become obvious that wasn't the case.

Robert had been in the Marines; he was a pretty strong fellow who I believe could hold his own. Nevertheless, he said he didn't know what to expect when Doug went over to the bar and said, "You black boys better get your butts out of here, or my friend and I are going to have to throw you out." Robert said all he could think was that he sure as hell didn't want to fight them. He didn't want any trouble with the local cops; plus, he had no quarrel with these men, although Doug apparently did. As luck would have it, the colored men simply shrugged their shoulders and left the bar. Robert said he vowed then and there he would never go anywhere with Doug again.

******

I got to know a lot of the old timers on the island. Many of them said the island had always been a strange place, long before it became the site of the nuclear generating station. Tales of hauntings, winds reminiscent of banshees, strange lights, and hobo camps were told in abundance. One fellow even told me his granddad had spoken of a time the island served as a refuge for slaves during the Civil War. Although sometimes at night, when the wind would blow through the air, thick with the rising mist from the river, it was a bit on the scary side, I mostly passed these tales off as folklore. Who could say if there was really any truth to them? I did believe them when they told me where the island got its name, though; there was some logic to the simple story that it was because of its location 3 miles south of the town of Middletown.

******

I befriended a fellow who lived near Middletown. He trained and raced horses at the Penn National Racetrack in Grantville. One night, he invited me to his house for supper. As I watched him have a horse swim a circle in the pond, I thought of my grandfather. I was reminded of how he could speak to the horses. I felt the same sudden calmness in that moment that I always felt when I was reminded his spirit was by my side.

A few weeks later, that fellow invited me to go to the track to watch his horse race. "Okay, why not," I said. At the track, we sat in the owner's box; he, of course, told me to bet on his horse. I thought I had to be in an old-time movie, where the race was fixed; but, I went ahead and bet $100.00 on that horse of his. I'll be damned if it didn't come in! I won $600.00; I even went down to the Winner's Circle and had my picture taken with the horse, the jockey, and his family. I still have that picture (*see illustration*). That was a good bet.

******

Jim was a competitor; he was always looking for a competition, he always wanted to win. There was this one night I remember distinctly. It was about midnight; we were riding our motorcycles down Route 22, a four-lane highway, back to the campground. Out of nowhere, he decided he just *had* to race me. It was the first time I ever rode a motorcycle over 100 mph. To this day, I will never let him forget that I beat him. Not exactly the smartest bet I ever took, racing at that speed; but I believe I had someone watching over me, protecting me.

******

Four of us dressed out for entry one Saturday and went into the auxiliary to do a simple job. Within maybe 5, 10 minutes, we began to detect a terrible, strange smell through our particulate masks.   Now, understand, the masks were designed to filter out radiated dust, but not to block odors.   The smell was horrible, it almost *tasted* metallic. We immediately aborted the entry and called for assistance from the HPs. They contacted the Hershey Medical Center; an ambulance picked us up at the rear loading dock as soon as we'd changed into civilian clothes. Sadly, no one at the Center knew what to do with us; they just put us into isolation. They kept us there for about 4 hours while doctors came in periodically to listen to our chests, nothing more; it was not too comforting. I told the guys they were just waiting for us to turn green, which, of course, was not received as "funny" at the time.

We never did get a straight answer about where that odor came from, or what the HPs thought it was when they called for the ambulance. The best I could figure was that radiation makes metal brittle and begins to break down its basic elements; so, perhaps, it was airborne radiation-contaminated oxygen? Either no one had the answer, or they were just not sharing it with us "common workers." Three of the guys on our four-man team from that Saturday left the island and never came back; probably smarter than me.

******

The days were long and the nights were lonely. I spent my days off at the movies, or prowling the antique shops and flea markets. There was a store in York that boasted itself the "World's Biggest Yard Sale"; it was there I met an old friend from Allentown dealing sports memorabilia. His name was Andy; he was a teacher at a Vo-Tech school. He invited me to his house later that night for some supper and to play some poker. It was at that poker game I met Jerry Rhome. Now, unless you followed college football in those days, his may not have been a household name; but, if you did, you would know he was the top-ranked quarterback in the nation in 1964. He played for the University of Tulsa where his successful career left him just

74 points shy of the Heisman Trophy; it was the closest vote ever for that honor. Rhome was drafted by the Dallas Cowboys. He eventually went on to coach 24 years in the NFL, even earning a Super Bowl ring with the Washington Redskins. He was a really nice guy, down-to-earth. Jerry's father was a coach and had made some NFL films on 8 mm back in the '40s; I just so happened to have a few of those films. I later sent them to Jerry; he was so grateful. He was quarterbacks coach for the Seattle Seahawks at the time; that Christmas, he sent my kids a large box of Seahawks memorabilia – books, cards, an autographed football, and a jersey signed and worn by their quarterback, Jim Zorn. To this day, we keep in touch. Just goes to show, you never know who you'll meet in life, or when you'll meet them.

******

The reactor room was opened early in 1980; a tech entered to measure the radiation and the heat index. He was the first human inside since the date of the accident; he was not in there very long, but long enough to pick up a good dose. It was a distant 6 months later when the first de-con team would enter that room. I was on that team.

There were still some "hot" spots to be secured around the airlock, but after months of making our way through the auxiliary, containing the radiated water, we had finally made it to the base of the reactor room. However small it was, we were making progress. The reactor room was lined with cork to insulate and cushion it from possible seismic events; the sump pumps were highly radioactive and had to be shielded. Neither the cork nor the sump pumps would ever be used again.

We were making our entries from near the turbine room, wearing special vests, but not dressed out quite as heavily as we had been in the auxiliary. The reactor room was the "hottest" place on the island, and it was huge. If you look at pictures of Three Mile Island, you will see two massive domed structures between the hyperbolic cooling towers; these were the reactor rooms. The years to come would prove us right on just how difficult we anticipated de-con and de-fueling of Unit 2 would be; the unit would never be used again.

Entries had become so routine, they were boring. As boys will be boys, ribbing and trickery became commonplace. I remember one Vi-Cam worker, a young, skinny kid from Boston, who spoke with a distinct accent. Well, the Rebs, the few remaining southern workers left on the island, just tormented him, constantly making fun of his speech and his size. On one particular entry, the Rebs packed him into a bag and put it into a 50-gallon waste drum. When I entered with another team on the following entry, about 20 minutes later, we found him in there, fast asleep. The kid was good-natured; he took their ribbing in stride.

******

I made the mistake of going with Lou to "The Tiger," a biker bar in Steelton. I have no idea what possessed me to go along with him; the place looked like it was straight off the set of "Hell's Angels." Lou had heard the girl he was chasing at the time worked there. "She used to," the motherly-type woman working behind the bar told Lou. I found out later that woman owned the place, and, she was, in fact, regarded as a mother-figure to the entire gang in that bar.

Well, we had stuck out like two sore thumbs from the minute we stepped foot in that bar, dressed in sport shirts while everyone else was leather-clad. Some of the guys in there were huge, looking as if they could be ex-NFL players. After the woman had responded to Lou, a "biker chic" approached the bar; the entire place got really quiet. The lighting was so dim, all I could see were the two guys playing pool in the corner; one of them was the largest mountain of man I'd ever seen. I wasn't sure what was about to go down, but I remembered again the bar fight Jim and I had been in a while back. I sure didn't want to repeat that scene. All of sudden, the alarm on that large fellow's wristwatch began to sound, playing "The Yellow Rose of Texas." Everyone laughed, the tension was broken.

We wound up playing pool with those guys; in fact, I beat them all. As we left, they all hollered after me, "Wahoo! You make sure you come back and visit us." Again, it just goes to show you never know who life will lead you to become friends with, or who will accept you as "one of them."

******

The health physics teams were made up of both men and women. For the most part, the women were responsible for manning the entry locations. They recorded the names and numbers of men on the entry teams, and they checked us out upon exit to make sure we hadn't gotten "crapped up" inside. Now, not only did several of the guys always manage to get "crapped up," having to strip down completely to shower, but, many of the guys dressed out naked and, so, on exit, were naturally naked. Well, some of those female HPs, being quite the flirts, started a chart on the wall to measure "the manhood" of the teams. Of course these ladies were just guesstimating, but they giggled to no end when they assigned the men to their chart in the categories "big man, medium man, average man, little man, mini man, or still-growing man." Our foreman, Robert, always went in naked, and came out broken-hearted when the ladies charted him a "still-growing man"; we, of course, laughed. After all, we appreciated anything that would break the tension.

******

To call this place "Fantasy Island" may have been more appropriate than "Three Mile Island," or so it would seem at times. I remember a boy from Nevada who had arrived on a big motorcycle with one of the later teams. On our way into the unit to help ready the holding tanks for spent fuel rods one morning, he told me he hadn't slept too well the night before. When I asked him why not, he told me he kept hitting his head on the gas tank? Well, it turned out some of the guys had worried him that someone would steal that bike of his; worried him to the point where he would take it to bed with him in his rented trailer. I just shook my head and laughed. Then, I found myself looking up at the huge overhead crane; finding myself transfixed by its size, my mind flashed back, once again, to a day so many years ago...to another memory more akin to fantasy than reality.

******

Struggling to keep my balance, I opened the door to the deck house; I half fell and half slid in that door. "You alright, boy?" the chief asked.

"I will be when we get to Bermuda, Chief. That is, *if* we get there."

"Have no worry, son. I have been in these storms before."

"Yeah, but you're an old Salt, I'm just a passenger."

"Not today, son, not today. Put on this life vest and tighten it real good."

"Hell, Chief, I won't need this if I slip and go over the side. You won't find me floating out there. Besides, it will make the climb all that much more difficult."

"I know, son, but you know the drill."

"Yeah, I know the drill," I mumbled, as I obediently tightened the straps. I followed orders. "Hey, Chief. There is another crane operator on board you know."

He laughed, "Yeah, but he doesn't have your ability or expertise. That's what happens when you're the senior."

"Hell, I trained him, he can do it."

"He's below decks, throwing his guts up," the chief chuckled. "Besides, aren't you the guy who always told me it was your job, and no one needs to do your work?"

"Yeah, but I was kidding." We were trying to make light of this ridiculous situation. I couldn't figure out what the hell I was going to do after I ventured up there on that crane. I had been in some hairy spots before, but nothing like this – ever.

The stern came churning out of the sea; the ship shuddered, as if it hung suspended over the water, until the bow moved up the next wave, pushing it back down. I could feel the expansion plate as it snapped with a loud bang. We went over the plan once more. I was to slack the hook cables so the chief and his two men could pull them out of the deck rings; then, the crane would be all in my hands.

I had run those cranes for the better part of 3 years. Once, in the Boston Harbor, while unloading live ammunition to an ammo barge, I couldn't see the hooks for 7 decks below as I brought the skids up; one slip and the entire harbor would have gone afire. But, the water was calm, the ship wasn't moving, I had an excellent signal man; there was relatively little to think about beyond the caution of the job at hand. We were an unbeatable team; but, now, in the middle of this hurricane, were we working against unbeatable odds?

As I opened the heavy steel door, the wind tried to blow it closed, almost succeeding. Pulling my knit watch cap down as tight as I could, I moved toward the railing. I peered out at the sea; the waves were enormous. If I had not been living this experience, I would not have believed it was reality. But, I was living it, I did live it, and it was as real as anything I've ever known.

The rungs that were welded to the bottom side of the crane were about 18 inches to a foot from the outboard railing; in fact, they were so close, you could step on one rung as well as on the top of the railing. That is how close I was to open space. Once I started up, there would be no safety net. As stressful a situation as this should have been, as this was, I was overcome by a sudden, familiar calmness. I thought of my grandfather; he was with me in that moment, my ever-faithful guardian angel. I could hear him whisper, "Don't ever be afraid, son. I'm here."

Like riding a bucking horse at a rodeo, I took hold of the first rung and started up. I was strong and in good shape, weighing 165 pounds and able to bench 200; my arms would serve me well. The rungs were wet, slippery and cold. I had left my gloves tied to my waist, wanting to feel my hands as they moved up each rung. I had to fight the temptation to race up as I would have had we been in port; my actions had to be deliberate. Just as I reached the crane tracks,[xxiv] as I was reaching up for the next rung, the ship lurched to starboard. I pulled my hand back and held on. Clinging to the rungs, getting beaten by the wind and soaked by the spray of the ocean, I was not a happy camper. I waited for the bow to start up the next wave, figuring it would push me into the body of the crane. I sure didn't want the stern to come up as the bow dipped; that would have thrown me clear of the rungs and the crane, leaving me to fight my own body weight. I knew the trick was in being in rhythm with the ship, keeping my "sea legs," so to speak.

I found my rhythm and reached the top of the control deck. It was slippery with oil residue and sea water. The railing was only waist-high; it would be easy enough to get thrown over. I reached to the control panel, turning to face it against the relentless wind, and flipped on the power. The motors came to life; I could barely hear them amidst that howling wind. If I couldn't hear those motors, I could forget being able to hear anyone from below; everything would have to be communicated by hand signals.

It was the middle of August, but my hands were cold; I finally put on my gloves. I turned to the pedestals. Mounted on those pedestals were the control wheels, four in all – one for rotation, one for boom, and two for the hooks; they were made of brass and measured about half the size of a car steering wheel. There were foot controls for the brakes at the base of those pedestals. Everything was wet, slippery and cold. I thought about just a month ago being in Guantanamo Bay, Cuba, where we could get brown just by stepping outside, and here it felt like we were in the dead of winter. Here, in Bermuda, in August, in the midst of Hurricane Ginger; and let me tell you, this storm was anything but *gingerly*.

As I looked out upon the sea, it was brutal; it appeared to be getting worse. Maybe it looked so much more violent than it had from the deck because I was up so high on that crane, but, believe me when I tell you, words cannot begin to describe what I was seeing out there. My imagination wasn't playing tricks on me, either; this was Mother Nature in all her fury. When the bow of the ship dove into the water, those waves looked damn high; they had to be 50-75 feet, higher than the ship. I tried to see the chief below, but he was near the bow of the motor launch. I couldn't make another move without support; if I went into business for myself with those 300-pound hooks, somebody could seriously get hurt. I mumbled to myself, "Come on, Chief, where the hell are you?"

Finally I looked down to find the chief waving up at me, signaling me to put slack in the hook cables. Cracking open the wheel just a bit, with one eye on the chief and the other on the hook cables, I began to let the cable go slack. Immediately the chief signaled for me to stop; I stepped on the brake and returned the wheel to neutral. I could see his crew struggling to free the hooks below, it would be difficult to wrestle those hooks under these conditions. If they couldn't open the clips, we'd have to lay the hooks down to take the weight off. So far, I hadn't been given that signal.

From all the years of running this monster, I had learned a few of the ship's own signals, some things you would never notice from observing her tied to a pier. Knowing these things made it easier to read the ship, to know how and why the crane, in particular, would behave. And, so, I knew before the chief even signaled to me, that the men had cleared the hooks because the crane had begun to slide along the top of the T-cradle. There was a certain amount of slack in the crane rotation because of the wheels, and, once free from the cradle, the crane would begin to buck on the tracks, almost like it was trying to throw me off. I raised the boom just high enough to clear anything below; bringing the hooks back up, tight to the boom, I began to rotate to my right to swing the boom over the deck rails.

Amidst the excitement, I remembered two other times I'd had the boom run away, once on the down side and once on the up side, both with the starboard crane. Hitting the emergency switches even failed to stop that out-of-control starboard crane, both times. The first time it got away, it crushed the 40-mm gun mount; the second, it came up until it hit the sheaves[xxv] at the top of the roller post. I was port side now; I had never had any trouble with this crane. I guess there is always a first time, though. If for some reason this one should run away in a downward motion, we would be in serious trouble. We needed a crane barge to come along side to lift the boom when that starboard crane had run amok. If this boom should fall now, with the ship rolling so violently in the angry sea, it could very well collapse the whole crane into the ocean. As I rotated the crane toward the sea, I thought to myself, "Hold on, grandfather, we're going for a ride." I felt that sudden, familiar calmness and knew he had been along for the ride even before that invitation.

When the rotation had put me over the outside deck rail, I raised the boom all the way up, as far as it would go. Then, I locked it. If it decided to run away, Lord only knows which direction it would decide to go. I wanted time to jump clear. As the ocean continued to slam into the ship, the crane continued to buck on the rollers. I was not concerned about the shaking, but I was concerned about losing the boom. The ship rocked with the ocean as the raised boom vibrated. The tight cables seemed to be humming in the wind. Once I had cleared the deck rail and boom, I stopped. I have run this crane thousands of times,

I thought. Confidence in my ability should have served to bolster my thinking; but, it was at this point I began to lose my indestructible machismo. You see, when we're young, we all seem to think we are greater than we are; as I looked out at that sea, though, I wasn't so sure anymore. Scared? Not exactly...just in need of a little reassurance. Almost as if on cue, I had the innate sense that I was not alone out there; I had someone who was keeping me calm and focused, as I always did in trying times. My guardian angel, my grandfather, reminded me he was right there by my side.

Jumping over 40 feet on a rolling steel deck wasn't an option; even if it had been possible, with all the equipment on deck, there wouldn't have been a clear spot to land. Climbing down the ladder wasn't an option; it had separated from the lower rungs. I had only *one* option, stay with the plan, whatever that might be. So, I waited for the next signal from the chief.

As time seemed to be standing still, I had the time to take in everything around me, to etch the scene forever in my mind. The stern of the ship was to my left. I could see the huge waves of water cascading off and over the rails. Turning my head slightly to the right, I could see the dark, raging ocean. The bow was turning fully as it struggled to hit each wave square. I thought about what a wonderful scene this would be to share with my kids and my grandkids someday; that is, I reasoned, if I survived to tell it.

******

"Old Ironsides," *The USS Constitution*, now there was a story to tell my grandkids, I remembered. I was lucky enough to steer her in the Boston Harbor a few years back. She needed to be turned around and tied to the pier in the opposite direction as she sat, allowing the weather to work both sides evenly. A seemingly innocuous task, but to me, it was an event. An avid fan of history, I had read about "Old Ironsides" on more than one occasion. Long ago, I had read how children collected pennies to save that ship; and, then, lo and behold, there I was at her helm. At the time, I wondered if anything could ever overshadow steering this historical ship. Just goes to show, you never know where life will steer you.

******

An enormous wave hit the bow, shaking me out of my daydream; this event would certainly overshadow just about anything. I looked for the chief aft, but he wasn't there. I looked to the bow and the deck below, still not finding him. Then, I looked to the deck house where I had been given my orders; it was there I finally caught sight of the chief, off to the side, waving frantically. I watched as he circled his arm in a rotating motion, understanding that he wanted me to bring the boom around to face the bow. I couldn't do this from the inboard side; I would have to continue the outboard route, rotating through the seaward side. Rotation on this crane wasn't very fast to

94

begin with, but it seemed to move even more slowly as I turned the wheel open as far as it would go. The old horse shuddered with each crashing wave. As I crossed the 90-degree angle to face the bow, I was hit full blast with wind carrying the salty spray of the sea. The wind was so fierce I had to grip the wheels even tighter to maintain my balance, lowering my head into it, trying to shield my eyes. The boom, being raised so high now, was taking a beating; its weight began to contribute to the rocking of the platform. This was getting scary. Finally, over the deck again, I felt a twinge of relief; even though I still couldn't climb down, at the very least, should anything have happened now, I was not out over the ocean.

After I had lowered the boom into a more controllable position, the chief signaled me to swing over the Captains' Gig.[xxvi] As I got into the lifting position, I wondered if this was the reason for the move; surely we were not going to abandon ship? If we were, no matter how the other crane operator felt, whether he was still below deck throwing up or not, he would have to go up on the starboard crane to lower the Admiral's Barge.[xxvii] Lowering a boat under these weather conditions, without the crew riding it down, would be a really bad idea, to say the least. There would be no way for me to bring the boat near enough the side of the ship for the crew to scramble aboard. The rolling ocean would swing the boat, crashing it into the side of the ship, possibly even crushing a crew member or two. We'd had that happen once before, by the way. We were tied to a pier as one of the steadying lines snapped, throwing the motor launch on its side; a young seaman had his pelvis broken. But, back to the present, if we were to abandon ship now, the crew would have a devil of a time releasing the hauling lines and hooks from the boat as she thrashed in the sea. The lifting lines running fore and aft, the small lines both port and starboard, they would all have to be released; the forward would be the most dangerous. Releasing it, as there is no place to stand without falling overboard, would mean a seaman would have to lie on his stomach and crawl along the deck. As the potential dangers of this scene ran through my mind, I knew the futile exercise would surely be the absolute last resort.

About 30 feet below, the hooks were banging into each other as they swung on their cables; it sounded like a clock tower tolling the hour. I watched as those hooks swung back and forth, pausing slightly as their course would change to fore and aft. I could tell the ship was now riding higher on the waves. Everything around me seemed to be vibrating. The smoke from the stack was blowing back across the deck; the guys in the engine room must have had the boilers wide open. As the stern came up, I looked ahead only to see the bow disappear (*see illustration*). I was momentarily fearful of the unknown, but I knew I had to stay calm; if I didn't keep my cool, the situation could only get more out of control.

Just then, I noticed the messenger on the quarter deck had come back to the boat deck to talk to the chief; the chief was nodding his head vigorously, hands waving in all directions. Suddenly, the ship rolled starboard, throwing me off balance. It was the nastiest roll we had ever taken; there was no time to prepare to weather it. Instead, I slipped, hitting the deck of the crane. I wound up on my stomach, between two motors, my arm just outside the lower rail, my life jacket wedging me in. Out of the corner of my eye, I could see over the edge to the deck below, but I could no longer see the chief. Looking up, I could see the mast arms; they looked like they were touching the ocean. The crane rocked and the boom shook. I lay there trying to gather my senses. Then, I began to check myself out. I moved my feet, then my left arm. I pulled my right arm in as far as I could. After wiping my face, I noticed my hand was red; my nose was bleeding, though I didn't feel it or remember banging it. Peering over the edge of the crane deck, I was again able to see the chief. He was right below me, in a panic. He was hollering to me, but I couldn't hear a word; the wind was howling like a freight train. Realizing he must have been asking if I was alright, I thought to myself, "How the hell do I know, Chief? I'm on my stomach with a bloody nose." No sense getting him any more excited than he already was, though, so I gave him the thumbs up. He took off his hat and wiped his brow. A few minutes later, I struggled to get to my feet. Wet shoes don't work so well on a greasy surface, though; they're even worse when trying to gain traction to get unstuck from between two very large steel motors. After some struggling, I managed to free myself and get up; the life jacket was a pain in the butt, but I remembered it was the same life jacket that cushioned my fall and wedged me in safely during that roll.

Standing up, I once again spotted the chief. He signaled I should put this baby back to bed; I was more than happy to oblige. Giving him the thumbs up, I began to bring the hooks back up and, then, rotated the crane toward the deck rail. Same drill as before; I started out toward the sea, lowered the boom into the cradle, and secured the hooks to the deck rings. I climbed down off that monster at least twice as fast as I'd gone up. The chief was holding open the door of the deck house as I came in. "Good job. I thought I lost you, son. You want a cup of coffee?"

"Only if you have a straw handy," I jested. He chuckled.

Gripping that coffee, I began to wonder if the chief really had any idea how close he came to losing a crane operator. The ship had turned hard right, but had the ship yawed left, it would have catapulted me right out into the ocean. I hadn't thought through that fully at the time, atop that crane; but, now, being able to catch my breath, the gravity of the situation was quite clear.

The chief commented, "You have blood on your cheek, are you hurt?"

"No, Chief. Just banged my nose on something."

"You want to go to sick bay?"

With all those seasick sailors up there, I thought not. "No, Chief. I'm fine." Then I had to ask, "Do you know why we did this, Chief?"

"Seems it was a drill, son. The Captain wanted to see if it could be done."

"Well, I sure hope he is happy. And I hope he took notes, so we don't have to do it again."

Amidst all the excitement, we did lose one member of our crew. A young cook slipped in the galley when the ship took that tremendous, sudden roll. He broke his neck. The carpenters aboard made a pine box for him; he was stored in the ice locker until we reached Bermuda.

We found ourselves in the tranquility of the storm's eye the next morning; it was like night and day. The serenity belied the evil of the storm. The water was calm, giving us time to regroup, to get some sleep and enjoy some hot chow. I went up on the boat deck and climbed the crane to polish up the controls. Reliving the surreal ride I'd taken up there the day before, I swear I could again feel my grandfather's calming presence; my guardian angel remained at my side. I remembered the day he took me to watch him whisper to the high-strung horse at the local auctioneer's farm, the day he first told me, "Son, don't ever be afraid of anything." I swore I heard him whisper those same words to me the day before, calming me amidst the high-strung winds and waves of the storm.

$$******$$

I ventured back to the "World's Biggest Yard Sale" in York one afternoon. It was a nice day, so I had taken my motorcycle. As I came up alongside a pickup truck, I noticed two guys were sitting among the construction materials in the bed; they were passing a bottle back and forth through the open rear window. It looked like there was a total of five guys in the vehicle; the two in the back started pointing at me. They'd obviously been drinking for a while. Now, I have been around long enough to sense trouble, so I backed off, giving them plenty of room. They, in turn, slowed down. As one of the guys in the truck bed reached for a 2x4, the other for a cement building block, I knew for a fact there would be trouble. There wasn't enough room on the side of the road to pull over safely. Turning around wasn't an option; it was a one-way street. If I tried to gas it passed them, they'd probably still have time to throw one of the objects out of the vehicle. I couldn't try to cross the median, I could flip the bike. I had no options. Finally, they stood up in the back of the truck, armed with the 2x4 and cement block. "Where was a cop when you needed one?" I thought.

The street narrowed as we approached the seedy part of town. If there was a red traffic light at the intersection up ahead, I'd be stuck. I would have nowhere to go, but to hang back as far as I could. I scanned the sidewalk, figuring, if push came to shove, I could ride up on it and go like hell. As I pondered the thought, I heard the distinct growling noise of a loud-piped motorcycle behind me. I glanced over as the bike proceeded to pull alongside me. Perched on that bike was the biggest mountain of a man I'd ever seen; and, yes, I had seen him before. I'll be damned if it wasn't the guy who'd befriended me in "The Tiger," the biker bar in Steelton. Here he was, along with his lady, who sat waving behind him. Boy, was I glad to see them. I motioned to the truck up ahead; he nodded, letting me know that he'd sized up the situation. Then, his girl handed him what turned out to be a gun. He rode up alongside the truck, waving the gun at the drunken boys. I reckoned they wanted no part of him; they floored that truck right down a side street.

My old pal slowed down until we were side by side, grinning now from ear to ear. He gave me the thumbs up and motioned for me to follow. I followed him to the bar and bought them all drinks. He gave me a big bear hug; his girl gave me a big kiss. I just shook my head and said, "Man, was I glad to see you."

"You're one of ours, Wahoo," he replied. "We protect our own."

Sure was nice to be liked, but I have to believe there was more to this incident. Was it fate? I'm not so sure. I believe there was even more to it than him being in the right place at the right time. The moment I saw his grinning face on the bike next to mine, I suddenly felt calmed. I knew that feeling, that sudden calmness. I believe my grandfather was, once again, there in that moment; I believe my guardian angel had guided my old friend to that intersection to protect me in my time of need.

******

The preferred drink on the island was rum. I never handled rum very well. We were on liberty and had rented some scooters at $6.00 for the entire day. The man who had rented us those scooters had a big Harley Davidson motorcycle of his own; we would find that out later in the day as he chased us down with it, looking to get his scooters back when we didn't return at the designated time.

The driving was interesting as the roads were narrow, with rocky cliffs that came right down to the berm of the highway. We stopped at a small café for lunch before the road began to circle back at the end of the island. Walking down the path to the white sandy beach, I stared out at the water; it was so blue and clear that I could still see the white sand right through that water. We sat at an outdoor table to take in the view, a view that was made even more pleasurable by some young ladies who were showing off their bikinis for the swabbies.[xxviii] We even enjoyed some rum.

I was driving my scooter as fast as I could on the way back to town, just having a good old time. Suddenly, I noticed a big truck was coming straight toward me, in the same lane. I thought the driver had to be crazy. I waved at him to get back in his lane, but, he wouldn't move. That's when it dawned on me that he wasn't in the wrong lane; *I was* in the wrong lane. I swerved at the last second, just barely missing him. That poor guy probably thought I was playing a game of chicken. I took a deep, calming breath, realizing how lucky I was. But, it wasn't luck; I didn't believe in luck. I had a guardian angel watching over me, my grandfather's spirit was with me on yet another wild ride. After that incident, I began paying much closer attention when driving.

The rum flowed freely straight through the evening, though I drank very little; I wanted to be cold-stoned sober when the rest of the guys were "sloshed to the gills." About 10 of us, from all parts of the ship, had gone out to a bar called "The Smuggler's Cove"; the bar was literally a cave. The entrance was at the end of a tunnel, the stone walls lined with old pirate cutlasses and hanging torches. Across the street was the Hotel Hamilton, the biggest, fanciest place in town; it had a big front lawn behind a gated entrance. Next to the hotel was an old prisoner-of-war ship from the 17th century; the water around that ship was full of barracudas.

We all knew each other well enough. One fellow, a 5'8" Italian boy from the Bronx had drank so much he could barely stand. Another decided it was a good idea to go swimming; that was about 11:30, an hour and a half before our 1 A.M. curfew to report back to the ship. Those guys ran across the street to the Hotel Hamilton, stripped down to their undershorts, and dove into the water; they dove right into the water next to the war ship. "You guys are nuts! There are barracudas in that water," I warned. I had no intention of joining them.

One of them hollered back, "No problem, they're all asleep!"

Tiring, they soon crawled up on the wharf and sprawled out on the lawn. Not long after, shore patrol showed up, got the boys dressed, lined us up, and took our liberty cards. We were directed to several taxi cabs that they had waiting to take us back to our ship. All the while, this one fellow, Mike, was complaining of stomach cramps, saying he needed to use the head.[xxix] Now, the cabs could only hold two guys apiece; Mike ended up in the cab in front of mine. As we neared the pier, I noticed Mike's cab was parked by the guard shack; all the doors were open, the cabby gesturing and hollering at the guard. When we got out of our cab, Mike was laying on the wharf, all curled up in a ball, sound asleep. The guy that had ridden with him was still in the cab, out light a light in the back. I looked in that back seat and began to laugh like crazy. Poor Mike had to use the head so badly, he hadn't been able to contain himself; like a baby with nasty diarrhea, he had gone all over the back seat of that cab, all over his buddy and his uniform, too. The cabby was furious, or so we assumed; we couldn't understand a word he was saying. He was from Trinidad, so upset he was no longer speaking English.

Four of us stripped Mike down, throwing his clothes and shoes in a barrel. He was buck-naked as we each grabbed an arm or a leg to haul him down the wooden pier, banging his butt every so often; but, he was out cold, not waking up once the whole way up to the quarter deck. The officer on deck wanted to know if Mike was alright. "Yes, sir, we'll take care of him." We carried him up to his quarters and dumped him in the shower; the water was ice cold. He woke up, beating against the steel sides of that shower and hollering like a banshee. Then, we turned on the hot water, watching him curl up and fall asleep. For 20 minutes we repeated this dousing, trying to get him cleaned. Finally, we laid him over the sink, toweled off his butt, and rolled him into his sack.[xxx]

Mike remembered nothing the next day; all he knew was he couldn't find his shoes or white pants. Needless to say, our liberty was cut short; water or no, we had to pull out. The captain was not a happy camper. The captain said we had embarrassed the Navy and ourselves, not to mention the flag admiral. Of course, it wasn't just our gang of 10; I had heard that some of the other guys had some trouble the night before, too. They'd driven their rented scooters off some cliffs, betting on which they'd hit, the ocean or the rocks.

We pulled out and headed for the North Sea en route to the Netherlands. It was 1957; as we started that journey, we heard the Russians had launched *Sputnik*.[xxxi]

Both the weather and the sea were calm as we got underway. We picked up our escorts and proceeded to the English Channel. Let me tell you, it felt like we were on a pleasure cruise after weathering Hurricane Ginger.

******

Strange things occurred at sea, especially in the throes of the Cold War. Our sonar picked up Russian submarines quite often; they liked to dog our ships. Sometimes a sub would surface within shouting distance, just pop up like some bloated whale. They became even more daring after the launch of *Sputnik*, trying to actually bump and run us a few times.

Our captain was an old Navy sea dog; he had done considerable time on a destroyer,[xxxii] and, once in a while, he tended to forget he was no longer aboard that greyhound, but a mere repair ship. One day a Russian sub surfaced near our bow. Sonar reported several more subs in the area. The surfaced sub opened its hatch and its captain emerged, shouting obscenities at us from a bullhorn. They were always harassing us, playing games. Well, our captain didn't cotton to their antics.

Distance on the ocean is short; a mile on land may be hard to see across, but, at sea, a mile is comparable to a short city block, you can see everything quite well. Off the starboard quarter was a ship that looked to be a fishing trawler. I moved over to that side to get a better view; I even got my camera, such as it was just a little Kodak brownie. I could see the hammer and sickle painted on the smoke stack of the trawler, as well as the fenders[xxxiii] hanging over the side; no ship sails at sea with hanging fenders, they are designed to tie up alongside other ships or to tie in next to a pier. Knowing the area was infested with subs, we assumed this was a supply ship that had been sent to service them.

After the emerged sub had nearly run into us, our captain was not a happy man. He turned our ship toward the trawler. We could see the stern as we approached, noticing it was not flying a flag. We knew she was Russian, we'd seen the hammer and sickle on the stack; but, the law of the sea holds that you must fly your flag to show recognition. A couple of us, standing amidships near the flying bridge, looked up to see our captain with a bullhorn of his own. "Strike your colors," he shouted. Then we noticed the woman aboard the Russian ship who stood waving at our captain. Not a good thing to do when he was mad.

Our captain entered the wheel house. The next thing I heard was the klaxon and boson' mate on the bridge. "General quarters. Man your battle stations. This is not a drill." As I ran to my gun station, I thought the old man must really be ticked off. I climbed up into the gun director's position, up to the 40-mm gun mount. I could make out 5 columns of smoke in the distance; our tin cans[xxxiv] were making knots. As we made a run at the trawler, sonar reported subs were leaving the area. The captain came out on the flying bridge, shouting, "Show your damn colors or I'll blow you out of the water."

Being higher off the deck, I had a good view of the action. The woman who had been waving at our captain had run up to their bridge and was now running back to the fantail, tying the hammer and sickle flag on the rope. After she finished hauling it up the mast, she turned her back to us, pulled down her trousers, and bent over to present her naked butt to us. Now, we may not have spoken a word of Russian, but we knew exactly what she meant to say. I laughed until there were tears in my eyes.

After securing from general quarters, we all wondered if the old man would have given them a broadside. Personally, I think he would have. Amidst all that confusion, I still managed to get one good picture with that Kodak of mine (*see illustration*).

We were not harassed by another Russian sub until we reached Norway. While anchored out there in the bay, one surfaced about 200 yards away; the captain just stood on the conning tower, saluting us. I often wondered if that was the same one from the incident at sea.

We were only anchored in that harbor for about 3 days before we received orders to move out. It would seem

Eisenhower had landed 5000 Marines in Lebanon and we were to join the task force for support. It was a shame we didn't get to spend too much time in Norway, though; it was, is, a beautiful country.

We went around the Shetland Islands, heading south. Sometime during the night we rendezvoused with the task force, refueled, and got in line, standing off as the Marines landed in Beirut. When I awoke at 5 A.M. the next morning, I stepped out on the deck; I had never seen so many ships in one location. This would be my last cruise. When we returned, I had only about 6 months to go on my hitch, or so I thought. Once again, fate, or something greater, would step in.

******

It had been established the core was in a "cold shutdown"; the pumps had held up long enough to do their job. The unit was now safely in natural convention circulation, using the natural movement of water without the assistance of the pumps. The plan was to insert a miniature video camera down into the reactor itself, into the control rod spacing, to ascertain the damage. This plan would require the removal of the heavy missile shield above the reactor, which, at the time, wasn't possible. The polar crane at the top of the reactor had been exposed to high levels of radiation, not to mention the accumulated krypton gas and burning hydrogen during the incident. That crane, which would have to be used to remove the missile shield, would first need to be tested and inspected itself.

Even though I was lucky enough to have met some people on the island who were pretty in-the-know, most of the information that reached us from higher up was well watered-down by the time we heard it. Without a clear-cut view of the incident, speculation was all that was possible. Buzz on the island had been there were two camps of thought at an oppositional standstill. Some assumed the fuel had melted and run down between the fuel rods; their thought was that the situation was not proportionate to a meltdown. Others suggested a "relocation of the neutrons," claiming the detectors toward the inner wall were reporting large numbers of neutrons, which would indicate a considerable amount of fuel lay at the bottom of the reactor; their thought was that the situation was, in fact, a verifiable meltdown.

At the very least, I was able to determine the reason for our maiden entry into the reactor room; it was to be "experimental." We were to dress out in ice vests weighing close to 30 pounds. The room was extremely "hot" and extremely humid; at 100 percent humidity, the temperature was higher than tropical ambient temperatures. We were to simulate tasks to see if it would be possible for future technical workers to withstand the conditions. Although one tech had already made entry to test the radiation levels, ours would be the first full-scale, active labor attempt in preparation for placement of the desired camera. It would still be a full 6 years before that camera would actually be sent down.

******

January 10, 1959. A mere 17 days to go; I settled in, looking forward to completing my final 4 years. A fellow in the engineering gang was having some trouble at home. We bunked in the same quarters; so, as it always seemed I was the one the guys having marital problems would talk to, we talked. Apparently his wife had taking a liking to some Marine. My bunkmate was a really nice guy; I felt sorry for him. I offered to take his duty Friday night so he could have a 72-hour pass to handle his troubles; I had such a short time to go, trading for the 48-hour pass didn't seem a huge sacrifice.

It was during those extra 24 hours aboard ship, readying for an all night pinochle game with a few of the other guys, the fire alarm sounded. As I was the one on damage control, I responded. Seemed there was a fire in a deck house that some of the crew had been painting earlier. A 5-gallon can of turpentine exploded as I entered that deck house, setting my left leg on fire. I stepped out the door, and, looking down, I can remember clear as day saying aloud, to no one in particular, "I'm on fire! My leg!" Before I could even pull my dungarees down to smother the flames, I had been burned straight through to the bone on my ankle. The corpsman arrived shortly after, wrapped my leg in cold, wet towels, and called the base ambulance.

For the next 4 months I would lay flat on my back; I would have 3 skin grafts.

At first, I was forewarned of the possibility my foot would have to be amputated. Fortunately, however, one of the countries' top skin care specialists at the time was stationed at the Newport hospital where I had been taken. He was a rear admiral, a tough red-headed fellow. I remember the nurse warning me not to show any pain when he came to examine me that Sunday morning. He stood at the foot of my bed, talking to the emergency care doctors. They had used an aluminum silicate powder to form a crust on my leg; he cut that crust off with a pair of scissors. Damn, did that hurt! I could feel the bottom of the scissor blade tear through the muscle tissue. I can honestly say it was worse than the fire. Holding the thin bars of the bed post, I remembered the nurse's warning. I wouldn't show any pain until after he left that room, but I sure did bend the bar on one of those bed posts while he cut. After he'd finished examining my leg, the rear admiral just looked at me and said, "Son, I'll see you in surgery tomorrow." The nurse told me I'd done a good job. I replied, "Thanks. Now get me some painkillers." She chuckled as she left; she returned shortly after with the pills.

I could do nothing in isolation except count the holes in the ceiling and think, a lot. I was stuck in there for 14 days riddled with staph infection after that first operation; my leg lay in a trough as a bag dripped acetic acid (pickle juice) over it. I watched as the nurses wheeled out bodies with sheets over their heads. To some extent, I was immune to all this activity; I never thought for one minute that I would not be just fine, that I would not be leaving here in one piece.

When my body was ready, I was able to undergo the second surgery; this one was successful. I was moved to another ward to continue treatment of the boils that had developed on my fingers from the infection; they were soaked periodically, and finally lanced.

During the 4 months I was stuck in that bed, not being able to so much as lay on my side, I amused myself by giving the nurses a hard time. I'd tell them they couldn't keep me in that bed, that I was "a Civilian." I learned to never say anything like that to Navy nurses; after that, they began to amuse themselves. They would wake me up at two o'clock in the morning just to give me sleeping pills, or two of them would bathe me simultaneously, scrubbing as hard as they could, chuckling the whole time.

The day finally came for me to swing my legs over the edge of the bed and stand upright. Well, I did that for just about one full minute before I fainted. Rehabilitating that leg took many years, but, at least, I didn't lose it. This leg of mine is still in working order, thanks to that admiral...and, I believe, my guardian angel. I remained calm and rational when I needed to, putting out the fire, staying positive when the doctors first told me I could lose that foot, rehabilitating my leg. I know that my guardian angel was the calming spirit by my side every step of the way, minimizing my pain. He had always been.

Others had it a lot worse than I. The fellow I had traded liberties with that weekend, well, he came back to the ship after his 72 hours. He came back to the ship, took a 45, wrapped it in a blanket, and shot himself. I thought to myself, "Hope that Marine had himself one good time; cost one man his life and messed up my leg." The twists and turns life takes us on are really strange.

******

The new style vests were frozen, and encased in plastic. The plan was to assimilate working conditions, moving around to work up as much sweat as we could. This would be "a different kind of painful," I thought, as we began to dress out.

Our entry could not be an extended one, as the reactor was emitting a ton of radiation; it was still extremely "hot." Everything in that room was radioactive, from the dust to the smallest pieces of equipment; we would have to be extremely careful not to compromise our suits or face masks. Each step of this operation had to be planned in detail; there could be no foul-ups. The eyes of the world remained on Three Mile Island; our operation here would set the course for future standards.

I often wondered during my time on the island just how I'd wound up here. Of all the men in our line of work, of all the events to be assigned to, how was it that I was chosen to participate in such a monumental undertaking? Was I fated to be here? Did my guardian angel lead me here, knowing he could protect me and keep me calm enough to protect some of the others? The answer still eludes me.

There was nothing a crew could do in the reactor room, and there wouldn't be for quite some time. We walked up the ramp, opened the outer door, and, then, closing it, checked each other's gear once again. We checked our dosimeters; mine was already registering - one was a 500-unit, the other a 1000-unit. We opened the inner door, and stepped down into the room. I stood there, thinking about the core; this was as close as I'd ever been to a nuclear reactor, not to mention one damaged beyond repair.

As I looked at the other two guys, each from different district offices, I realized, at least, why I'd been put on this particular detail. One fellow was short and stocky, the other tall and thin; I was the biggest. If this was to be an assimilation of work force, the company must have wanted to see just how each body type would react. What else could it have been? Sure, I had probably made more entries than most to-date, but anyone could have made this entry for mock procedure. The higher-ups didn't like to explain their logic, so, as I've said before, an awful lot was left to speculation. Maybe I was over-thinking the reasoning for this entry, but what I was thinking sure seemed plausible. In that moment, I knew how a guinea pig must feel.

The reactor room was a man-made marvel of science. For the last 2 years, it had been the subject of much worldwide attention. It would forever be etched in history; in some small way, my being here had made me a part of that history. That thought was awesome. I scanned the room, noticing the very same melted red phone that I had seen on the news when the story of the incident first broke, when I was just another spectator. I walked over to place my hand against the wall of the reactor.

Trying to breathe was becoming increasingly difficult. Even with the ice vests, the heat was stifling. The air was so humid; it was like being in a sauna with a clothes pin on your nose and cotton stuffed in your mouth. My lungs began to hurt as I tried to suck in more air; I could feel my heart pounding. The last time I checked my dosimeter, it had been off-scale. I placed my hand to the ice vest; feeling it had turned completely to water, I suddenly realized I'd lost track of how much time we'd been in there. We gave the signal that we were coming out. Future entries would have to be of shorter durations; it was apparent no one could do much in here for very long. Instinctively, our movements slowed under those extreme conditions, under those same extreme conditions in which our instincts had to remain sharp.

May 14, 1981. I turned to take one last look at the monster as we climbed the stairs to the exit. Closing the door, I was fully aware it had been my last entry. We were never given exact counts, but I was told that I had picked up, at least, about 3600 milirems of radiation, over half the yearly allotted dosage, during that single entry.

******

I have been asked my thoughts on nuclear power many times over the years. Being a layman, I cannot, with a good amount of technical parlance, debate, or even begin to explain, the intricacies of fusion. I can, however, offer some common sense evaluations about the nuclear industry.

As with anything under government oversight, there tends to be a great deal of political interference in the industry, with patrons ending up in jobs for which they are perhaps not the best qualified. Though the incident at Three Mile Island may have allowed scientists to enhance safeguards for nuclear plants and to fine-tune their crisis manuals, the warranted concerns and fears of the public are no less apparent today than they were in the wake of that fateful morning.

An end to the debate over the safety and effectiveness of nuclear power is not something I foresee in my lifetime; perhaps, dear reader, not even in yours. In my humble opinion, nuclear power will never displace or conserve oil; it will never preserve our coal resources. We, as a country, regardless of the potential for use of nuclear power, will continue to consume exorbitant amounts of these natural resources, saving less and less for future generations. I remember my grandfather's admonition, "Son, take only what you need and save the rest; pass it on to your needy neighbor." Idealism never sounded so good.

******

I believe each and every one of us has his or her own story; a story of a lifetime of trips and falls, hardship and joy. Some of our stories are filled with nothing but elation, others with nothing but heartache and fear. I believe your life should have a mix of it all; you need one to enjoy the other.

I have tried to live my life by my own quote, "Hardship is the fire that tempers the steel in your backbone." I resolved a long time ago to never point back and blame my upbringing for the actions I might take in life. It was the proverbial falling and getting hurt that taught me to get up and cope. I have shared these very same sentiments with my own children and grandchildren. I find the tendency to over-protect children in today's society to be quite sad. As a parent, the trick is to let them fall, but, then, to be there, holding out your hand to help them up, knowing that with each fall they will get stronger. Each fall will steel their backbones, teaching them they can survive. I'm living proof.

Although I didn't have someone to take my hand physically after my grandfather died, he was always there with me; and, he taught me how important it was to extend that hand to others along the way. I remember him telling me, one afternoon as he spoke to those horses, "Son, never be afraid to mount a bucking horse, so long as you have an understanding with the horse that you can jump off." Life is all about taking chances. Sometimes you need to have the courage to admit when the ride gets too rough; but, you also have to be brave enough to get back up on that horse to try again. My grandfather's words have echoed through my mind for as long as I can remember; I can still feel his hand holding mine. I have never been alone.

Today, my life has come full circle. I work for the Catholic Church, an organization from which I was ex-communicated over 50 years ago. I am awaiting orders for my next entry, the greatest adventure of all; the adventure that will reunite me with my grandfather.

******

All my life I have wondered just how or why I was taken down a road with so many remarkable twists and turns. I have wondered how my journey was driven. Was it by fate? Was it by the will of a higher being? Or, did I have a guardian angel watching over me? Against considerable odds, I have survived some extraordinary circumstances. The answer, I have decided, is that I could not possibly have survived alone.

I strongly believe there was a thread woven into my life, gingerly pulling me together and pulling me through. I strongly believe the thread in my life has been the ever-faithful presence of my grandfather, as a spirit or guardian angel, bringing me a sense of sudden calmness in my times of need.

[i] The core is the part of the reactor housing the stainless steel fuel rods which contain the fuel necessary for the nuclear chain reaction (i.e. the continuing process through which the nuclei of uranium atoms are split).

[ii] Coolant is the fluid, usually water, responsible for carrying the heat caused by the nuclear chain reaction away from the core.

[iii] Zirconium cladding refers to the long metal tubes which house the nuclear fuel pellets.

[iv] A meltdown is a catastrophic event in a nuclear reactor; the result is the potential release of massive amounts of radiation into the ground.

[v] Health Physics, or HPs, are scientists who focus on radiation physics and radiation biology. We called them "house pets."

[vi] The reactor dome is the container housing the core.

[vii] "Entry" is the term used to facilitate entrance to a radiation contained "hot" spot.

[viii] The vessel head is the top of the reactor.

[ix] The gloves we were issued were rubber, with tight, elastic fittings; multiple pairs could be worn at a time depending on a worker's comfort level or job.

[x] In traditional Irish folklore, a banshee is a spirit whose wail is foreboding of death; the animated wail of the banshee sounds similar to that achieved by blowing gently across the top of an empty soda bottle.

[xi] Face masks, or particulate masks, were form-fitting with a small window and a twist-on charcoal cartridge over the diaphragm. The charcoal cartridge was about the size of 2 stacked decks of playing cards; very difficult to breathe through.

[xii] A dosimeter is a device used to measure absorbed doses from exposure to radiation.

[xiii] Fred Waring was a popular local Pennsylvania musician/bandleader.

[xiv] A milirem is $1/1000^{th}$ of a RAD. RAD stands for Radiation Absorbed Does; the term is commonly used to measure radiation taken in by the body.

[xv] Starboard is the right side of a ship; port side is the left.

[xvi] A rack is the term for a bed on a ship.

[xvii] "Zoomies" was the term we used to describe radioactive dust and dirt.

[xviii] A hydrolyser is a high-pressure water hose, used to knock down radioactive dust and dirt.

[xix] "On the carpet" is slang for being summoned to review an incident.

[xx] About 4x4", with radiological instrumentation imprinted on a yellow background, step-off pads were taped to the floor with duct tape, lining the path out of the unit. Each one was designed to guide you to the "clean" area; we called them the "Yellow Brick Road."

[xxi] Fusion is the release of nuclear energy by the bonding process of atomic nuclei like hydrogen; it is the opposite of fission, which is a nuclear reaction achieved by the splitting of the nuclei of atoms.

[xxii] "Crapped up" was the term we used to indicate contamination.

[xxiii] Booties were the plastic covers worn over the rubber boots of a worker; multiple pairs could be worn at once.

[xxiv] The crane tracks are where the ladder rungs separate so the rotating wheels on the track will allow the crane to turn a full 360 degrees. That spot is usually greasy from the lube on the track.

[xxv] Sheaves are steel wheels at the top of the crane.

[xxvi] The Captains' Gig is an enclosed motor boat equipped with radios and survival gear.

[xxvii] The Admiral's Barge is similar to the Captain's Gig, only bigger.

[xxviii] "Swabbies" is slang for sailors.

[xxix] "Head" is slang for toilet facilities.

[xxx] A sack is a bed.

[xxxi] *Sputnik* was the first robotic spacecraft launched to orbit the Earth; its R-7 launch vehicle was initially designed to carry nuclear warheads.

[xxxii] Destroyers were submarine hunters during wartime; dubbed "greyhounds of the sea" because of their speed.

[xxxiii] Fenders look like telephone poles with tires strung down the length. The ropes at each end tied through chocks on board the ship.

[xxxiv] "Tin cans" are destroyers, in sailor lingo.

Photographs from my time in the U.S. Navy.

Top Left: in uniform, stationed in Cuba. Top right/middle: My ship, the *USS Yosemite AD19*. Middle Left: Our ship awash in the Bermuda Triangle. Middle Right: Our ship in port. Bottom Left: Russian trawler. Bottom Right: Crane aboard ship.

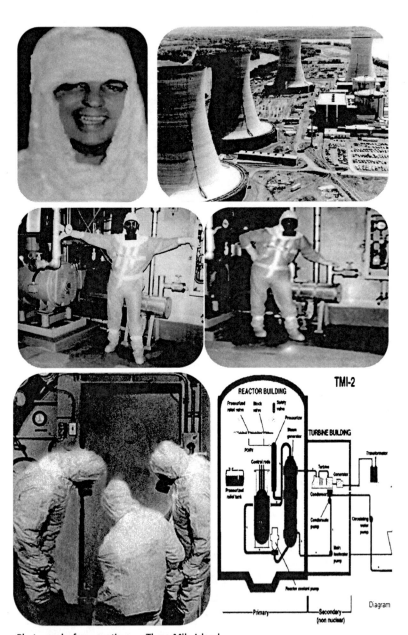

Photographs from my time on Three Mile Island.

Top Left: Dressing out for entry. Top right: Aerial view of the facility and cooling towers.
Middle: Fully dressed out for entry. Bottom Left: Preparing for entry. Bottom Right:
Simple schematic of the reactor, as discussed in the text.

Top Left: In the Winner's Circle. Top right: In uniform. Middle Left: My wife, Mary Ann. Middle Center: My granddaughter, Sydney. Middle Right: My grandson, Zachary. Bottom: My three children, Cynthia, Richard, and Kristine.

LaVergne, TN USA
28 July 2010
191219LV00005B/62/P

9 781589 097018